This journal belongs to

....

Inspired by the WORD

A CREATIVE DEVOTIONAL JOURNAL *for* WOMEN

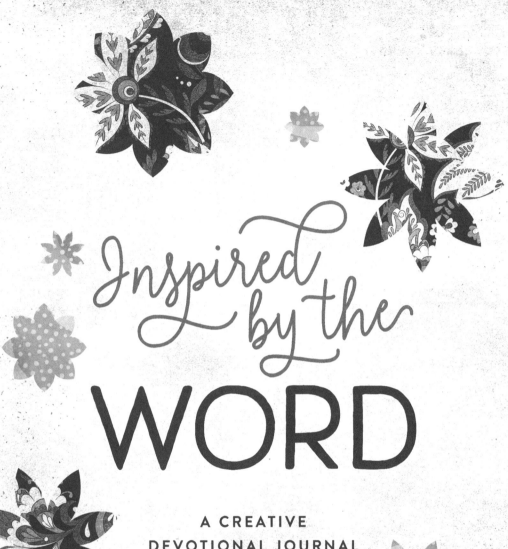

Inspired by the WORD

A CREATIVE DEVOTIONAL JOURNAL *for* WOMEN

VALORIE QUESENBERRY

BARBOUR
PUBLISHING

© 2019 by Barbour Publishing, Inc.

Print ISBN 978-1-63609-130-3

Scripture quotations are taken from the King James Version of the Bible.

Cover design: Greg Jackson; Thinkpen Design

Published by Barbour Publishing, Inc., 1810 Barbour Drive, Uhrichsville, Ohio 44683, www.barbourbooks.com

Our mission is to inspire the world with the life-changing message of the Bible.

Printed in China.

Be Inspired by THE WORD!

This lovely devotional journal—created with you in mind—will enhance your faith as you spend quiet time in the heavenly Creator's presence. One hundred words—including *peace*, *wonder*, *miracles*, *heaven*, *purpose*, *celebrate*, and more!—alongside inspiring devotional content and memorable Bible passages from the beloved King James Version of scripture will inspire you to think more deeply on the heavenly Father and the truth of His unchanging Word.

BE OF GOOD COURAGE, AND HE SHALL STRENGTHEN
YOUR HEART, ALL YE THAT HOPE IN THE LORD.
Psalm 31:24

"Hope springs eternal," says the old adage. Sounds wonderful, doesn't it? Like a tender sprout emerging from the soil, hope pushes up through our doubts and dismal prospects and tendencies to despair. Despite the sod weighing down on it, the seed of life rises, poking up through the dirt as though it were meant to be there all along. Hope cannot be squelched, boxed in, or buried. It will continue to be what the Creator intended—buoyancy of spirit and the bright allure of tomorrow.

Of course, the hope that the psalmist endorses is hope in the Lord. This hope gives courage and strength, not just a fanciful wish for rainbows and flowers. This hope is rooted in something solid, a never-ending source of nourishment—the eternal God.

One of the most difficult environments in which to hope is a hospital waiting room. When my youngest brother was lying in a trauma unit in an Indianapolis hospital after suffering a severe head injury and ruptured pelvis, my family had little to lean on but hope in God. Every change in the nursing shift brought changes— some good, some not good. His condition was unstable for a long while. He teetered on the edge of death and then on the brink of disability. Despair reached for us, its ragged hands coming at us from every angle. Perhaps you've encountered the same thing in a surgical ward or a nursing home or a funeral parlor. Maybe you looked despair in the face during a phone call from an adult child or in a conversation with a friend or in a moment of conflict with your spouse.

Know this: No matter the setting, there is always hope in the Lord. Despair is from Satan. Those who hope in the Lord are never forsaken.

_____

_____

_____

_____

_____

_____

_____

_____

_____

_____

_____

_____

_____

_____

_____

_____

_____

_____

_____

_____

LORD OF HOPE, GIVE ME EYES TO SEE BEYOND THE
CIRCUMSTANCES, EARS TO HEAR YOUR SPIRIT, AND A HEART
THAT REFUSES TO LET GO OF HOPE IN YOU. AMEN.

TRUTH

AND YE SHALL KNOW THE TRUTH,
AND THE TRUTH SHALL MAKE YOU FREE.
John 8:32

Truth is black and white and sometimes red. Have you ever been in a situation where the truth was hidden, kind of shady? And it wasn't a situation where you could shout out the real story? It was one of those "wait and let the truth come out" kind of deals.

Truth will come out in the end, it is said. This phrase is based on a sentence from *The Merchant of Venice,* written by William Shakespeare, referencing the facts about a murder. If there were ever a time when truth is most important, it is in those moments of determining guilt. At times like that, the truth is as stark as a vivid black-and-white photo from the past. It cannot help but be seen.

Yet there are times when truth is red—it waves a red signal to flag down everyone who starts to inquire about it. At those times, truth wears her bold colors, and no one dares make her change.

Jesus said the truth will set us free. Not just any truth, but His truth. And without Him, there is no truth of any kind. All we know of this world and ourselves and our place in it is because of the enlightenment He gives. Many sources claim to be truth. There is no shortage of news organizations, blogs, tabloids, and podcasts that aim to be *the* source. But when it comes down to it, only the One who made the worlds and upholds all things really knows the truth.

HEAVENLY FATHER, THANK YOU FOR BEING TRUTH AND FOR
MAKING ME FREE WHEN I PUT MY TRUST IN YOU. AMEN.

WHOSOEVER BELIEVETH IN HIM SHOULD
NOT PERISH, BUT HAVE ETERNAL LIFE.
John 3:15

When I found our black kitten dead in the backyard on the morning we were to leave for a family vacation, I thought again of what life means. Certainly, the life of an animal is different from the life of a human being. Animals are God's creatures, for sure. . .but we, men and women, bear His image. We are endowed with souls, a never-dying core that is defined by our choices and is expressed by what we do in our bodies. Whether we experience eternal bliss or torment is up to us. The animals, on the other hand, have no choice; they are made to glorify God by being and doing what their species does. Only to men and women has the Creator given the amazing opportunity to be in relationship with Him and, as the Westminster Catechism says, "to enjoy Him forever."

As I looked down at the fluffy little animal that we had enjoyed so much, I felt anger toward another of God's creatures who probably killed Sequoia (my daughter liked this name for the word *black*). But again, this is the way of nature, cruel and twisted as it now is because of sin's curse. And though I knew this little black kitty would return to the earth and become part of the fiber of tomorrow's soil, I still grieved for the pain of death that has passed on to all of us.

But I rejoice in the knowledge that not one of those who bear God's image has to perish—be dead forever. Those who put their trust in Christ, God's provision for our salvation and reconciliation, will go on living for eternity. That is the promise of the Gospel, the Good News. The ground is not our long home; we are made for another time and place.

CREATOR GOD, THANK YOU FOR MAKING A WAY FOR US
TO GO ON LIVING. I PLACE MY TRUST IN THE SACRIFICE
OF YOUR SON AS MY WAY OF SALVATION. AMEN.

ENTER INTO HIS GATES WITH THANKSGIVING,
AND INTO HIS COURTS WITH PRAISE: BE THANKFUL
UNTO HIM, AND BLESS HIS NAME.
Psalm 100:4

*Thankful. . .*it's a popular word today. It appears in decorative script on wooden signs, chalkboards, and even painted on pumpkins around harvest time. We can always use the reminder to be thankful. Human nature is quite prone to the opposite. We see it in ourselves more often than we like to think.

But *thankfulness* isn't just a trendy word for signage or a theme to embrace at the Thanksgiving table. Being thankful is a life attitude—an ongoing choice. And it begins with recognizing our God as the Giver of all good things and properly acknowledging the blessings He continually allows in our lives.

We are to enter His gates with thanksgiving, says scripture. Commentators seem to agree that this means to come joyfully into the place of public worship. In ancient times this would have been the gates of the temple; today it could refer to our sanctuaries. The courts of the temple were the places where worshippers would stand to worship. These times of worship should be the high points of our thankfulness. We can be grateful any day and time of the week, but when we enter His house, we should clothe ourselves with thankful hearts. And we won't even need it on a sign to remind us.

LORD GOD, WE LIFT UP OUR PRAISE TO YOU. WE'RE
GRATEFUL FOR OUR LIVES, OUR FAMILIES, OUR BLESSINGS,
AND MOST OF ALL FOR YOUR SON. AMEN.

BUT THE FRUIT OF THE SPIRIT IS LOVE, JOY, PEACE,
LONGSUFFERING, GENTLENESS, GOODNESS, FAITH.
Galatians 5:22

---

*Love. . .*it's a word we use every day in so many ways. Love can describe a spectrum of emotion from mere fondness to deep commitment. We often use the word in a casual way, and that's okay to a point. It's part of our twenty-first-century American verbiage, and it's often awkward to insist on exacting language in our day-to-day lives. On the other hand, it's important for us to know what love really is and what it isn't.

As a mom, you may have found yourself faced with the question "How do you know when you love someone?" Talk about the challenges of motherhood! Try defining that to your child. Even as you're talking about seeking the other's good above your own and wanting to commit to a lifetime with that person, you realize some of the deep aspects of love can only be understood in the context of real-life experiences. Real, tested love happens over time, and it takes some negative turns as well as positive. Yes, most of us realize that love is much more than a feeling. But it does include feelings; we all like that part.

The love that the Holy Spirit wants to develop in us is not so much about emotion as it is about action. God is very concerned with what we *choose* to do. He looks closely at the set of our will. He knows that emotion is like the temperature outside—subject to the forces of life, the stimuli around us, the fluctuation of our body chemicals, and the impact of how others treat us. But our actions are purely the result of internal decisions; and when we belong to Christ, He begins to put within us that divine motivation to "do unto others." And it is something we can *will* to do in any situation.

GOD, THANK YOU FOR THE LOVE YOU SHOW TOWARD
ME EVERY DAY. I ASK YOU TO LOVE OTHERS THROUGH
MY WORDS AND ACTIONS. IN JESUS' NAME, AMEN.

17

BLESSINGS ARE UPON THE HEAD OF THE JUST.
Proverbs 10:6

"Have a blessed day!"

"Too blessed to be stressed!"

"More blessed than I deserve!"

There is no shortage of phrases using the word *blessed*. It has exploded onto the social scene and is now used by Christian and non-Christian alike. I'm not sure who unbelievers credit with the blessing, but they do acknowledge that they receive good things in life. And that's positive. It can only be good for our culture to recognize blessings.

Blessings, though, should point us to the Bless-er. And He has set down certain eternal principles about blessings. Just like the laws of gravity and motion and mathematics, the laws of blessing work every time.

One of those principles tells us that blessings shower upon the just. The word *just* here describes those who are righteous, the ones who are living in fellowship with God. While God certainly blesses those who are rebellious and unrepentant, His intentional goodness is laid up for those who are in relationship with Him, just like an earthly father saves his best for his own children and not just the ones in the neighborhood.

Of course, we do not serve God for the stuff. That's the wrong motivation. It evokes the same feeling in us as an adult who only calls and visits his dad because he wants the inheritance someday. That's not relationship; it's manipulation. And it probably makes God feel the same way it does us, though He is big enough and holy enough that He continues to do good even to those who "use" Him.

Still, the point remains that the blessing He loves to give is reserved for those who call Him Father and who have been given eternal life through His Son. I hope that you're part of that family.

LORD, YOU BLESS ME IN SO MANY WAYS. I'M SO GLAD
TO BE IN RELATIONSHIP WITH YOU. AMEN.

PRAY

IN THE MORNING WILL I DIRECT MY PRAYER
UNTO THEE, AND WILL LOOK UP.

Psalm 5:3

All over the world, lots of people pray—and to many different gods. But the only prayer that is genuine communication is prayer to the one true God. The other kinds of "prayers" are just wishes and yearnings and petitions that go nowhere; they are not received by any power, and they only give the evil one more insight into how he can torment deceived souls.

Prayer to Jehovah God is a lifeline of communication and relationship. We can pray emergency prayers and relaxed prayers, short prayers and long prayers, choppy prayers and flowery prayers. If we pray with repentant hearts and in Jesus' name, we may be assured that our prayers do not fall flat but rise beyond the ceiling and walls to the God who is everywhere.

The psalmist says he will pray in the morning. It's a wonderful thing to direct your early-day thoughts to the One who made you and loves you like no one else. This kind of morning greeting needn't be stilted and formal. Maybe you think *Good morning, Lord* as you swing your feet onto the floor and reach for your bathrobe. Maybe you cradle your coffee mug, look out the kitchen window, and whisper your deep thoughts to the One who didn't need to wake up. And then maybe you find a quiet spot in the living room or on the sunporch and welcome the day in His presence.

Then again, perhaps your morning prayers must be lifted to Him while chauffeuring children to school, weaving to your job through morning traffic, changing baby diapers, or assisting an elderly parent. However you offer up your morning to Him,

He is glad when you do, and there is no substitute for His company anywhere.

....

....

....

....

....

....

....

....

....

....

....

....

....

....

....

....

....

OH GOD, I DELIGHT IN THE TRUTH THAT I CAN COMMUNICATE WITH THE
GOD OF THE UNIVERSE, WHO IS ALSO MY FRIEND. I LOVE YOU. AMEN.

Faith rests on nothing and yet is as strong as steel pylons. Faith in God, that is.

The eleventh chapter of Hebrews is often called the faith chapter, and for good reason. The names and stories recorded in it make up an amazing list of situations where God came through for His people. These folks were just like you and me in many ways. They were human; they had emotions and families and hardships and joys. They came up against huge obstacles in their walk with God, and they overcame them through faith.

Faith believes when there is no supporting evidence. But it believes not in magical appearances in answer to our wishes but in the truth that God Almighty will do what is best, what is right. It is faith in Him not faith in a specific answer.

Of course, many times the prayer of faith is centered on a specific request. If you read Hebrews chapter eleven, you will understand that these heroes of faith trusted the God who had promised. And they received. In His time. And what He ordained.

- Noah and his family were rescued.
- Abraham became the father of many nations.
- Sarah bore a child.
- Moses led his people out of bondage.
- Rahab was spared and given a place in Israel.
- And on and on.

Of course, some who believed were not spared suffering but were given the reward of triumphant faith—the eternal presence of God.

So, win or lose, success or failure, good or bad, faith is victory. This faith reaches out on nothing and accomplishes everything. This faith is in the God who is more substantial than the very ground on which we walk.

OH GOD, LET ME PUT MY TOTAL FAITH IN YOU AND IN YOUR POWER
TO DO WHAT IS RIGHT IN MY LIFE AND FOR MY FUTURE. AMEN.

Now this is a word I really enjoy contemplating. Perhaps it's because I was raised with an awareness of the afterlife, and heaven was discussed in joyful and expectant tones in my home. But I realize that not everyone had that same upbringing. For many, the thought of eternity and even of heaven brings fear and, at the least, apprehension.

My mother often says, "If God can make this life that we think is so wonderful, just imagine what heaven will be like!"

That's a pretty good way to look at it. Heaven is the better world, the upgrade to this one. Since God made us for relationship and family and celebration, and to enjoy nature and beauty and music and creativity, I really believe it's possible all those things will be in heaven. Heaven is not going to deprive us of what we enjoy now. Rather, it's going to give us undiluted, untainted joy.

If you're familiar with older hymns and gospel songs, you'll recognize that many of them talk about heaven. It seems that people of past generations enjoyed thinking about and singing about heaven. It was partly because their daily lives were harder than ours. They didn't have many of our comforts or our health care or our life expectancy. They knew that this life wasn't all there is. Today, we have lost sight of how good that other world will be. We can easily forget that our present world is cursed and broken until we get the unexpected diagnosis, the frantic phone call, the bad news report.

If you need a little good news today, rejoice in the fact that heaven is waiting for those who trust in Him. In today's verse, Jesus told His hearers to "leap for joy." Now that sounds like a kid getting an ice cream cone on a hot day! But heaven will be so much better than that!

LORD, I'M SO GLAD THAT HEAVEN IS MY ETERNAL
DESTINATION SINCE I HAVE PUT MY TRUST IN CHRIST. I'M
LOOKING FORWARD TO ALL YOU'VE PREPARED. AMEN.

Every one of us wants joy. And there are many Christian books and Bible studies on the topic. We've heard all the explanations and tried the equations, but joy often still eludes us.

Maybe we're looking for the wrong thing. Joy can be a feeling. It's an awesome one. But joy can also be a conviction, an assurance that God is in control, a sacred delight in the truth that He holds all things in His power.

Let's not relegate joy to just one of these definitions. It can be more than one, can't it? The God who made us knows that sometimes our emotions are engaged and sometimes they're not. So I think He gave joy a fluid nature so that it would fit where we needed it.

Paul, the apostle, could say he had joy in a Roman prison, chained to a guard. It might have been a positive emotion, but I rather suspect his joy was more of the conviction type.

Miriam, the prophetess, had joy when she celebrated with the other women on the banks of the Red Sea after Pharaoh and all his host were drowned. Her song of triumph is recorded in Exodus 15. This was most certainly a feeling.

The psalmist proclaims that he will be joyful in the Lord and specifically in His salvation. You can never go wrong here. Finding either or both assurance and emotion in the sacrifice of Jesus and the redemption He offers is a win every time.

Keep studying joy. Do those Bible studies. But just remember that joy is within reach, in one of its forms, wherever you find yourself. That's a pretty great thought.

LORD GOD, I WANT MY JOY TO BE FOUNDED IN YOU.
THANK YOU FOR THIS GIFT THROUGH CHRIST. AMEN.

GIVING

What do you think of as a symbol of giving? Could it be a red kettle? Yeah, you know, like the ones the Salvation Army uses at Christmas. If ever there were a visual for charitable deeds, that would be it. And we expect everyone to be a little extra nice during the holidays. Giving to help others then is part of the routine, an appropriate tradition to observe. And thank God for organizations that offer relief and assistance!

Yet giving is a year-round proposition, and God loves it when we love to give. Maybe that's because He is the ultimate Giver, and He delights to see His nature in us, like parents find joy in seeing their positive traits reflected in their children. When we love to give, we are imitating the One who was glad to send His Son for our redemption. Isaiah 53:10 says that it "pleased the LORD to bruise him." This does not mean, of course, that the Father delighted in His Son's suffering from a sadistic nature but rather that His perfect sacrifice made sense to the Godhead and that the Father approved and was satisfied with His Son's substitutionary death.

So when we give, we are imitating the One who gave first and gave best. And giving in His name is an act of worship. We can give money. We can give our time. We can give our space, showing hospitality and love. We can give in many ways. And every time we do it with a spirit of joy and excitement, we look just a tiny bit like our heavenly Father, whom we can never outgive.

....

....

....

....

....

....

....

....

....

....

....

....

....

....

....

....

....

....

....

....

FATHER IN HEAVEN, THANK YOU FOR GIVING YOUR BEST
FOR ME. HELP ME TO REFLECT YOU BY GIVING EAGERLY
AND JOYFULLY TO OTHERS. IN JESUS' NAME, AMEN.

THEN WAS OUR MOUTH FILLED WITH LAUGHTER,
AND OUR TONGUE WITH SINGING.
Psalm 126:2

Do you think Jesus laughed a lot? He was called a friend of sinners. Those who are not religious generally do not enjoy being around a stodgy, somber person. I think that Jesus was not only warm and kind but also humorous and friendly. Many of His teachings have humor woven into the telling. And I can just imagine that He and His disciples enjoyed fun times together, as would any group who stays around each other very long in ministry.

Laughter has been scientifically proven to be healthful for the body and the mind. God, our Creator, put this principle into the laws of our world. And that tells us something about Him as well. He is a God of joy and celebration. The scripture tells us about the feast days He commanded Israel to keep and relates how there is joy in the presence of the angels over a repentant sinner. We know that He likens the events surrounding His second coming to a wedding, a time of wonderful happiness. And over and over, He compares Himself to a Father who delights in His children. These things tell us that God Himself, holy and perfect, is a Being of eternal and unending and complete joy.

It is true that life often gives us situations about which we can't smile. It would be foolish to pretend that life is, as the saying goes, "a bed of roses." Nonetheless, we can cultivate a spirit of joy by reaching out for the humorous and the positive, by relishing good clean fun, and by remembering that heaven is the eternal answer to earth's questions. I want to be like Jesus. I want to honor my Creator by embracing laughter.

LORD, THANK YOU FOR GIVING ME THE ABILITY TO LAUGH, TO USE MY PHYSICAL BODY TO EXPRESS HAPPY EMOTION. I CHOOSE TO GLORIFY YOU BY USING THAT ABILITY TODAY. AMEN.

MY GRACE IS SUFFICIENT FOR THEE: FOR MY
STRENGTH IS MADE PERFECT IN WEAKNESS.

2 Corinthians 12:9

Strength is a word our world respects. From strength training in physical exercise to being strong in the fight against cancer, the concept is applicable in myriad ways in our culture. We see it illustrated in various mediums and forums. Trendy slogans, human rights campaigns, medical research, and even greeting cards all laud the attribute of strength of character and determination.

The apostle Paul was given God's opinion on strength. He was wrestling with a weakness, a limitation of some kind. For years, Bible scholars have debated the exact nature of his problem. We still don't know for sure, but whatever it was, it was debilitating in some way, and Paul did not have the power on his own to fix it. So he did what Christians do. He called on God. He asked the Lord to take away this hindrance, this infirmity.

And God answered no. Paul was told that he must continue in his ministry and trust that the God Jehovah would keep him going through divine power. Grace is divine enablement, and God promised it in abundance to His servant Paul.

He was further promised that God's strength would be clearly evident in his own weakness. That's how God shines clearest. In the darkest hour, the Lord's child can be a voice of testimony to His all-sufficiency.

What are you facing today that requires extraordinary strength? What battle demands power? What relationship needs support? What situation dominates your prayers?

Come to Him, remembering that "they are weak, but He is strong." Find that His strength is endless. Especially when you're weak.

....

....

....

....

....

....

....

....

....

....

....

....

....

....

FATHER, I'M GLAD THAT YOUR STRENGTH IS AVAILABLE TO
ME AT ANY HOUR AND IN WHATEVER QUANTITY I NEED.
GLORIFY YOURSELF IN MY WEAKNESS TODAY. AMEN.

WORSHIP THE Lord IN THE BEAUTY OF HOLINESS.

Psalm 29:2

Beauty is a message about God. All types of beauty—human, animal, botanical, celestial, aquatic, geographical—ultimately point to the Creator.

Satan, the enemy of God, knows this very well and does everything in his diabolical power to mar the beauty God has created or to twist it and use it for evil. The curse that passed on to our earth because of sin brought the principle of death into our world, and that death affects beauty. The laws of genetics that God put into place are tainted; plant life can be stunted, animal life deformed, human life disabled and maimed. The onset of decay incrementally disfigures beauty both in our natural world and in us. The natural disasters that occur because of disrupted weather patterns, ecological problems, and the horrific tragedies that take place through the sinful choices of man all destroy the beauty that God continues to create on our earth. Yes, the result of our broken world is the devastation of beauty.

Nevertheless, the beauty that remains, despite the onslaught of the curse, is a testament to the majesty of Jehovah God. He is the One who dwells in perfect and beautiful light. He put a shadowy reflection of His radiance into the planets and the oceans and the mountains. He lent a speck of His glory to the fields of wildflowers and the crash of the Niagara and the waving of the grain. He infused His spark into the frisky colt and the playful kitten and the excitable pup. He let us see His own image in the fresh velvet of a newborn's skin and in the wide-eyed gaze of a little girl.

And so He calls us into personal holiness. Beauty cannot live long without protection. Its delicate aura must be protected from the elements. We also need that protection. Our souls cannot withstand the assault of the enemy. God beckons us to draw close to Him, to surrender ourselves to His power. When we do this as an act of worship, He purifies and consecrates us, and we can begin to see the beauty of holiness in us. And it's something Satan cannot touch.

FATHER GOD, I WANT TO BE BEAUTIFUL IN PERSONAL HOLINESS.
TAKE MY BODY, SOUL, AND SPIRIT, AND PURIFY THEM AND
PRESERVE ME BLAMELESS FOR YOU. IN JESUS' NAME, AMEN.

FOR WHATSOEVER THINGS WERE WRITTEN AFORETIME WERE
WRITTEN FOR OUR LEARNING, THAT WE THROUGH PATIENCE
AND COMFORT OF THE SCRIPTURES MIGHT HAVE HOPE.

Romans 15:4

Comfort is a warm drink, a plush throw, a reclining seat, a hot meal, a tight hug, a listening ear. The things that comfort us are the things that minister to our human needs—physical and emotional.

The absence of comfort has defined many great saints of the past as well as many today. The biographies of missionaries are filled with accounts of struggle, of doing without, of being bereft of common means of comfort. The inspiring tales of the apostles and other early followers of Christ describe torture and imprisonment and martyrdom. The plight of fellow believers today in distant lands is punctuated by abandonment and poverty, abuse and deprivation. Even Jesus, our Lord, did not have a home of His own, though He enjoyed the hospitality of special friends in

Bethany. I wonder if Martha knew His favorite meal and tried to fix it when she knew He was coming? I wonder if Lazarus and Mary knew Jesus' favorite game to play and looked forward to conversation on favorite topics or about certain hobbies?

Comfort is what all of us enjoy and need. And God's Word tells us that scripture can give us comfort. Just like a fragrant cup of coffee on a chilly morning, the Word energizes us and challenges us and invigorates us. Or like a warm quilt, it envelops us and covers us and soothes us. The things written within it help us learn what God is like and how He works in our world, and through that knowledge, we become more patient and we experience comfort.

May you be blessed with a comfortable place in life today with all the little amenities that bring you joy. But know that the greatest serenity comes from the comfort found in the Word. Take advantage of that today!

....

....

....

....

....

....

....

....

....

....

....

....

....

....

LORD, TODAY I NEED COMFORT FROM YOUR WORD. YOU KNOW
THE PLACES IN ME THAT NEED YOUR TOUCH. SPEAK TO ME
THROUGH YOUR SCRIPTURE RIGHT NOW. IN JESUS' NAME, AMEN.

TRUST IN THE LORD WITH ALL THINE HEART;
AND LEAN NOT UNTO THINE OWN UNDERSTANDING.
Proverbs 3:5

Trust is the oxygen of relationships. Without trust, there can be no forward motion, no energy, no fulfillment. Just as the physical body has no life without oxygen, neither does a relationship. Without it, there is gasping, struggle, and death.

Earthly relationships symbolize great truths about the relationship God wants to have with us, though many times we become more enthralled with the symbol than the actual. The great theme of romance is the story God is writing about His pursuit of humankind. And He lets us see it in thrilling color through human courtship and marriage. A man and woman in a healthy romantic relationship have trust in each other; they have committed to seeking the other, affirming the other, and serving the other. They trust each other to value the relationship and to prioritize it above others. When there is mutual trust, there can be mutual love.

God asks us to trust Him. He desires a personal relationship with us. And because He is divine and we are human, He understands that we have incomplete knowledge of His ways and nature. He has shown us who He is through His Word and through His Son. Now He says, *"Trust Me and don't rely on your faulty insight. I have proven that I am trustworthy. Just read the stories in the Bible. Read about My Son. This is who I am."*

Trust allows the struggle of life to cease. Today, turn toward God with a trusting heart, and experience the calm that begins as the oxygen fills that relationship and brings back the glow of life.

....
....
....
....
....
....
....
....
....
....
....
....
....
....
....
....
....
....
....
....
....
....

FATHER GOD, I WANT TO TURN FROM ANXIETY TO TRUST IN
MY RELATIONSHIP WITH YOU. FILL ME WITH THE BREATH OF
YOUR VERY LIFE AND WORK YOUR WILL IN ME. AMEN.

FOR HIS MERCIFUL KINDNESS IS GREAT TOWARD US:
AND THE TRUTH OF THE LORD ENDURETH FOR EVER.

Psalm 117:2

Kindness is the basis of human virtue. To be kind is to think of others. It requires selflessness. And that strikes at the heart of the human condition.

We are inclined to be self-absorbed. Since the Fall and the entrance of sin, our human natures have been inverted to point toward self rather than toward God and toward others. So, when we follow Jesus' command to be "kind one to another," we are aligning ourselves with the intent of God for us—living in loving relationship with others (Ephesians 4:32).

This command flows out of God's very nature. He is kind, mercifully kind. He has proven it in myriad ways, both big and small. He grants us life, He allows the sun to shine, He gives us breath, He lets us experience love and family and friendship. And the greatest expression of His everlasting kindness was His gift of His Son to the world. Through that selfless and sacrificial act, God demonstrated just how great was His kindness toward us. He isn't willing that any of us be separated from Him, so He provided reconciliation through Jesus if only we receive it.

Because He has been so kind to us, we are to pass on His kindness in our dealings with others. We are to be kindness ambassadors to the ones He allows into our lives on a daily basis. There is no situation so irritating or so awkward or so tragic that we cannot show kindness. Yes, it will take courage and grace. And that's what He gives.

Be kind in His name today.

LORD JESUS, THANK YOU FOR GIVING ME AN EXAMPLE
OF WHAT KINDNESS SHOULD BE BY THE LIFE YOU LIVED
ON EARTH. I ASK FOR YOUR GRACE TO WORK IN ME SO
THAT I CAN BE KIND TO OTHERS TODAY. AMEN.

Salvation

THE Lord IS MY STRENGTH AND SONG,
AND HE IS BECOME MY SALVATION.
Exodus 15:2

Salvation is the theme of the Bible. And it's a total makeover concept.

The salvation God offers us is not a little bit of goodness added to our natures, but a total transformation of our entire being from the inside out.

Some theologians have referred to this idea as "full salvation." The Bible itself gives us this impression when it says in Hebrews 7:25 that Jesus is "able also to save them to the uttermost that come unto God by him." The Greek word translated *uttermost* here means complete or entire. Jesus didn't come from heaven to give us a halfway redemption; He came to redeem and renew every part of ourselves and our lives.

I am sometimes amused when I wonder what our culture in general thinks about the Christian organization known as the Salvation Army. Begun by General

William Booth over one hundred years ago, this charitable entity offers relief to the total person; assistance is given in both practical and spiritual ways. But I wonder if most people think that "salvation" merely refers to escaping poverty and abuse?

Jesus offered this type of deliverance for the entire person. It's the truth of His earthly ministry, and it was always the intent of God from the beginning. That's one of the reasons for all the many lifestyle laws in the Old Testament. God wanted a redeemed people, transformed and set apart in every area.

Don't let anyone tell you that there is a part of life about which God is not concerned. The Bible does not teach that. He is our salvation, our full salvation.

FATHER GOD, YOU ARE MY LIGHT AND MY SONG AND MY SALVATION. CONTINUE TO MOLD ME IN YOUR IMAGE AND TRANSFORM ALL THE AREAS OF MY LIFE. IN JESUS' NAME, AMEN.

GRACE

Ephesians 2:8

If we could earn grace, it wouldn't be grace. It's a gift. It's God's to give. It's the lavish bestowment of His favor and mercy on us when we deserved punishment. The Bible speaks often of grace. The apostle Paul often began and ended his letters to the New Testament churches with a blessing of grace to his readers. It's a concept that is totally and completely divine. Satan would never give any favor; he takes, he consumes, he destroys.

We see grace demonstrated very clearly in our culture every Christmas. The toy drives for underprivileged children, the free dinners at city shelters, the meals and coats for the homeless, the red kettles on the street corners, even the gifts under our own Christmas trees are all little bits of grace to others. We don't usually give Christmas gifts because someone earned them or even because they deserved them. We give them out of the favor in our hearts for them. And if we give for the right reasons, we don't give to get something in return. We give for the joy of giving.

God, from whom all grace and favor flows, extends His grace to us so that we can experience His salvation in our hearts and His empowerment in our daily lives. This grace is a rich gift that we only need receive and apply.

FATHER IN HEAVEN, THANK YOU FOR YOUR ABUNDANT GRACE
TO LIVE IN RELATIONSHIP WITH YOU. MAKE ME A CHANNEL OF
THAT GRACE TO OTHERS TODAY. IN JESUS' NAME, AMEN.

Contentment

BUT GODLINESS WITH CONTENTMENT IS GREAT GAIN.
1 Timothy 6:6

Godliness isn't something we hear advertised. To most people, it no doubt has a vintage, "uncool" vibe. But to the people who realize what really matters in life, godliness is what they want most of all.

Look at it this way: God made us. We were made by Him for relationship with Him. Being in total sync with Him makes us our best selves—we are the most fulfilled when we are in harmony with His will for and in us. This is essentially what godliness is. Seen from that perspective, godliness is the key to real happiness.

Added to that is the choice to be content. A person doesn't have to have total perfection in order to be content. In fact, if everything is perfect, the feeling of satisfaction one has is just a result of all the slots being filled, not of any personal strength of character. But contentment is a virtue that requires personal choice and will.

Paul wrote in Philippians 4:11 that he had "learned" to be content in any situation.

This is the result of continuing to mature in one's faith and understanding, as well as in the discipline of one's will. Contentment is not an emotion but a decision that can be made anywhere in any circumstance. And writing to his son in the faith, Timothy, Paul gives us a spiritual math lesson: Godliness plus contentment equals great gain (success).

_____

_____

_____

_____

_____

_____

_____

_____

_____

_____

_____

_____

_____

_____

_____

_____

LORD, I YIELD MYSELF TO YOU TODAY. I WANT TO BE IN COMPLETE RELATIONSHIP WITH YOU. AND I ASK YOU TO GIVE ME THE GRACE TO MAKE THE DAILY CHOICE FOR CONTENTMENT WHERE YOU HAVE PLACED ME. AMEN.

PRAISE

What is your love language? You've likely heard of this concept, which has been very popular in Christian circles when discussing relationships. Verbalized beautifully by Dr. Gary Chapman, there are five areas of expressing love that touch all of us in some way. Many couples and families have found this idea revolutionary as they learn to relate better to one another.

Each of us is unique and feels love more deeply in one or two ways than in others. The awesome thing is that God, our Creator, knows all about this and is able to speak clearly and powerfully to us in the way we hear it best.

One of the love languages is words of affirmation. While all of us enjoy positive words, some of us are more responsive to this way of expressed love. Affirmation has become a buzzword in our culture. We are reminded in many ways that we need to properly and positively affirm those around us. And, in a way, that is a type of praise. Yet the praise we are to give to the Lord goes beyond affirmation.

Praise to our God is not to build Him up and help Him feel loved. Rather, it is to acknowledge the absolute greatness of His character and works; it is praise that is His due. When we praise or affirm fellow human beings, we often overlook their flaws and focus on their good points. And sometimes we put the best spin on their actions and words. But we need never do that with God. He is always and eternally worthy of our praise. Whatever He does is always right, always best. And that is why we can pledge, with the psalmist, to praise Him with our whole hearts, without reservation, with complete confidence and joy.

LORD, YOU ALONE ARE PERFECT AND HOLY. YOU ALONE DO ALL THINGS
WELL. TODAY, WE PRAISE YOU WITH OUR WHOLE HEARTS. AMEN.

FOR HE REMEMBERED HIS HOLY PROMISE.

Psalm 105:42

Promises. They are whispered on moonlit nights by young lovers. They are uttered in delicate tones at the marriage altar. They are gasped out at the bedside of the dying. They are cherished and remembered in good and bad times.

Promises are dear to us. Often, they are a deep part of our most precious relationships. Inherent in family is the often-unspoken promise to be there for one another, to stick together through everything, and, if the family is a Christian one, to meet again in heaven. A husband and wife build a life together upon the promise that they will forsake all others and be a couple until death. Friends know that the unwritten rule of true friendship is to be available when things are not good and, when they are not so good, to seek the good of the other person even when that person is making bad decisions or floundering.

God has made promises to us. In fact, His Word is filled with promises. And He will keep every one of them. He began His work on earth through men and women of faith who became the nation of Israel through Abraham. The promises in the Old Testament were first made to them. And then through the redemptive work of Christ, all peoples and nations were welcomed into the family birthed by God's grace.

The very first promise God made to humankind is found in Genesis 3:15. He promised us that He would send a Redeemer to crush the head of the serpent. And He did just that on a dark day in Jerusalem when the God-Man, Jesus Christ, bowed His head on Golgotha and uttered, *"It is finished."*

Because He kept that promise and all the others, we are certain that He will take us one day to live with Him if we believe on His name.

....

....

....

....

....

....

....

....

....

....

....

....

....

....

....

OH GOD, WE ARE THANKFUL THAT YOU KEEP YOUR PROMISES. WE KNOW WE CAN TRUST YOU WITH OUR LIVES AND WITH OUR FUTURES. WE STAND TODAY ON THE PROMISES IN YOUR WORD. AMEN.

PEACE

BUT THE MEEK SHALL INHERIT THE EARTH; AND SHALL
DELIGHT THEMSELVES IN THE ABUNDANCE OF PEACE.
Psalm 37:11

An abundance of peace sounds like a summer evening on the front porch, sipping a cool drink and watching nature put on her dusky splendor. It's that feeling of tranquility, of all being right with the world and having the leisure of sitting to enjoy it.

But to imagine that we experience this kind of emotion constantly throughout our lives would be foolish. No one, Christian or nonbeliever, has feelings of unending calm. Life brings stress on many levels, and it's impossible to live for very long without finding that out.

So what does the Bible mean when it says the meek will have abundance of peace?

The meek are those who trust in God's strength, not their own; they are those who allow God the privilege of control and vengeance, who look to Him for the next step. The ones who are marked by this perspective will delight themselves in this peace, a confidence that there is nothing beyond His sight, His reach.

This kind of peace is not dependent on the weather, the season, the relationships in our lives, the kind of day we've had, the amount of money in our bank accounts, or the condition of our homes. All of these things can add or detract from feelings of peace, but they cannot actually take away our peace, this peace that is confidence and trust.

We are human. We are emotional. We enjoy good feelings. There is nothing wrong with that. But the truth is, feelings are fleeting; they are dependent on what is happening in us and around us. This abundance of peace can go on in spite of our feelings. That's a wonderful thing.

GOD, OUR FATHER, WE WANT TO EXPERIENCE THIS DEEP
ABUNDANCE OF PEACE IN OUR LIVES. SHOW US HOW
WE CAN TRUST YOU MORE FULLY SO THAT OUR PEACE
GOES DEEPER THAN OUR CIRCUMSTANCES. AMEN.

I WILL REMEMBER THE WORKS OF THE Lord: SURELY
I WILL REMEMBER THY WONDERS OF OLD.
Psalm 77:11

Imagine a child's eyes on Christmas morning or a native of a third-world country at a banquet. Remember the first time you saw the heavens in a planetarium or your first glimpse of the ocean expanse.

Our God is a Worker of wonders. We don't have to go very far to know this is true. The Genesis account of Creation is the obvious place to start. There is plenty of place for wonder there. The One who spoke things into existence is surely great. When He uttered those words "Let there be. . . ," there were birds, flowers, fish, animals. These natural wonders, with all their intricacies, appeared when He spoke.

Another time in scripture when the Lord performed wonders was during the days of Israel's slavery in Egypt. God had commanded the pharaoh to let the people go, but he would not. So God, knowing the superstitious nature of the Egyptian mind, put on a display of His power, stunning the heathen ruler and his court with the ferocity and intensity of His acts. From turning the waters of the Nile, the lifeline of their agriculture, into waves of blood, to causing hail and deadly bolts of lightning to decimate the cattle of the land, from hiding the sun for hours until people were going mad, to sweeping over the kingdom and striking midnight death to the firstborn, Jehovah demonstrated that He alone had supreme authority and power over this world.

Many miracles are recorded in scripture, both in the Old and the New Testaments. Over and over the Lord has shown His ability to intervene, to heal, to resurrect, to rescue and redeem. These events should not make us demand that He work in the same way every time but rather should help us to keep alive in our hearts the wonder of the God we serve and to trust in Him even more fully.

DEAR LORD, I AM AMAZED AT YOUR POWER AND MIGHT.
I HAVE SEEN YOU WORK IN MY OWN LIFE IN WONDERFUL
WAYS. THANK YOU FOR BEING A GOD OF WONDERS. AMEN.

NO MAN CAN DO THESE MIRACLES THAT THOU
DOEST, EXCEPT GOD BE WITH HIM.

John 3:2

Miracles are visible proof. They symbolize deeper truth. They are sometimes valued more than truth.

Jesus often performed miracles in His earthly ministry. For a populace who was not highly educated and did not have the benefit of scripture in their hands, these signs helped to confirm that He was who He said He was. The average person in Jesus' day did not know the fine points of God's plan of salvation (it all hadn't even happened yet!), but they did know some of the basic prophecies about the promised Messiah. And one of those was that He would perform miracles. So Jesus' acts of healing and resurrecting helped to establish His identity with the common people.

Does God perform miracles today?

Yes, He does, but it seems that often He uses medical science and other types of advances to accomplish them. While this may not be as awe inspiring to us, it is no less the result of God's hand, since He alone gives men and women the intelligence and ability to discover and create and develop technology and medicines and industry.

We live in an age of information and revelation as well as a day of modern advances. We have the scriptures in many mediums, in many translations, and for most of us, in multiple copies. We have the Holy Spirit to open our eyes to the truth about Jesus. We don't need miracles in the same way and for the same reason as those who lived in ancient times did. God still does miracles, and we are awed and grateful when He does, but He has the authority and wisdom to decide how and when to intervene in our situations and emergencies. We can trust Him to do what is best.

....

....

....

....

....

....

....

....

....

....

....

....

....

GOD, THERE IS NO MIRACLE TOO HARD FOR YOU. AND YOU
KNOW HOW TO WORK BEST IN MY LIFE. TODAY, I ASK YOU TO
BE THE SOVEREIGN LORD OVER ME. IN JESUS' NAME, AMEN.

CREATE

IN THE BEGINNING GOD CREATED THE HEAVEN AND THE EARTH.
Genesis 1:1

Many of us trace our first creations to a finger painting displayed on our mom's refrigerator. Even at preschool ages, human beings like to create, to watch something emerge from their hands. We get this love from our own Creator in whose image we were made.

Those who deny that our world and everything in it came about by intelligent design are missing an explanation for the creative spark that resides within them. While some minds might futilely speculate that the world could happen by chance, they can find no satisfying reason for the instinctive need they feel to invent and fashion and produce. This urge is the direct result of the divine spark within us.

God is the Master Designer. We only know about the creation we can see and read about in the record of the Bible. But how do we know what amazing things He has been creating from infinity? A creative God who is eternal will be eternally creative. There is no end or limit to His power to bring forth beauty and wonder.

Just look at the facts about the details God has put into insect life and plant life and even into the cells of our very bodies. Such intricate parts and exacting rhythms can boggle minds. If God can do this in only six days, just imagine what He has been doing from eternity past.

....
....
....
....
....

CREATOR GOD, I STAND IN AWE OF YOUR MIGHTY WORKS
OF CREATION. I THANK YOU FOR THE WAY YOU DISPLAY
YOUR GENIUS IN OUR WORLD, AND I LOOK FORWARD TO
SEEING WHAT YOU'VE DONE IN THE NEXT ONE! AMEN.

INSPIRE

MY HEART STANDETH IN AWE OF THY WORD.
Psalm 119:161

You need inspiration to live. Well, maybe not to keep breathing, but to really "live," inspiration is necessary. One of the Old Testament prophets wrote that without vision, the people perish. There could probably be many interpretations of this verse, but it is very true that a goal and a feeling of anticipation are needed for us to have any kind of zest for life.

God intended that His creation around us, His breath in us, and most of all, His love for us would inspire us daily. We were made to be active, to have purpose, to enjoy His gifts. When sin entered our world through the rebellion of Adam and Eve, negative influences began to assault the inspiration we needed. Now we must look beyond the circumstances around us and upward to our Lord for inspiration. He does not change, and His purposes remain constant.

One of the unchanging ways He has provided for our inspiration is His Word. His laws and precepts are true; His accounts of history past can be trusted; His admonitions teach us how to live; and His promises give us confidence. When we take time to read His Word, we are not only investing in the most important relationship we will ever have, we are also giving ourselves a dose of inspiration for the day and even the week ahead. There is always cause for hope and joy in the words of scripture. Hope because He will be with us in everything and give us grace to overcome. Joy because our future is settled if we know Him and because we are loved eternally and redeemed fully through His Son, Jesus. Yes, the Word is the inspiration you need today.

LORD GOD, SPEAK TO ME THROUGH YOUR WORD.
INSPIRE ME TODAY TO LIVE A LIFE THAT PLEASES
AND HONORS YOU. IN JESUS' NAME, AMEN.

CALM

HE MAKETH THE STORM A CALM.
Psalm 107:29

It always frightened me. As a child, I had Bible stories on short-play records. Yes, those were the old days. There was a matching picture book with a page for every story. Without fail, I would run to my mother when I came to the page of the storm on the Sea of Galilee. For one thing, the music was scary to match the mood of the storm. And being small, I didn't like the idea of storms either.

Things haven't changed much. While I'm not terrified of storms, I don't relish them. And since I've lived in parts of the country where weather can get very severe indeed, I tend to be leery of low-hanging clouds and greenish skies. My family once rode out a hurricane in central Florida; I still remember that howling wind and the staccato sheets of rain.

There are some who like thunderstorms, enjoying the flash of lightning and clap of thunder from the safety of their front porch or picture window. But not many of us would enjoy a storm at sea. The towering waves and foaming troughs do not seem pleasant in the least. We know that sudden storms arise even today on the Sea of Galilee, where Jesus and His disciples spent much time together. I'm sure the fishermen would have waited if they had known the weather would turn violent.

But they had the great Peacemaker aboard. Just as the psalmist predicted in this verse hundreds of years before, Jesus commanded the wind and waves to be still, and scripture says there was immediately "a great calm" (Matthew 8:26).

Do you need calm today? What storm has whipped up in your path? Never fear. He can bring the calm.

JESUS, THANK YOU FOR BEING THE PEACEMAKER. I'M GLAD YOU ARE
LORD OF MY LIFE. GIVE ME CALM TODAY IN MY STORM. AMEN.

BLISS

TRUST IN. . .THE LIVING GOD, WHO GIVETH
US RICHLY ALL THINGS TO ENJOY.
1 Timothy 6:17

I think of spas and luxury soaps and pampering. That's what bliss sounds like to my indulgence-craving imagination. And it is true that there are times when we unexpectedly receive what could be termed frivolous blessings.

But the blessings to which this verse most likely refers are not those so monetarily extravagant that they induce guilt; they are blessings that are rather costly from the standpoint of heaven's calculations. Everything we enjoy is a gift that has to come, in some form, from God. Even the ability to take pleasure in sinful indulgences is a result of the way we are wired and designed. This does not mean that God intends for us to snatch pleasure however we can, but it does tell us that the very existence of pleasure is because He willed it to be so.

It follows then that the gifts themselves are also what He wills into being. These gifts include every good thing in the human experience, from family to sweet tea, from cheesecake to go-karts. God is the instigator of joy, the One behind every wholesome laugh and hearty chuckle, the benefactor behind every full tummy and delighted sense.

This is what bliss really means. It isn't guilty pleasure but rather pure joy in the things He provides. And when these things are taken away, God is doing some other work in us. He gives and He takes away, said Job, who certainly experienced more than his share of loss, it seems to us. Yet he trusted in the God who withholds for our good and who restores in His time. We should do the same.

LORD, I RECEIVE YOUR GOOD GIFTS WITH OPEN HANDS. HELP
ME ENJOY THEM AND USE THEM AND RELINQUISH THEM WHEN
YOU BRING A NEW SEASON TO ME. IN JESUS' NAME, AMEN.

HOME

IN MY FATHER'S HOUSE ARE MANY MANSIONS: IF IT WERE NOT SO, I WOULD HAVE TOLD YOU. I GO TO PREPARE A PLACE FOR YOU. AND IF I GO AND PREPARE A PLACE FOR YOU, I WILL COME AGAIN, AND RECEIVE YOU UNTO MYSELF; THAT WHERE I AM, THERE YE MAY BE ALSO.

John 14:2–3

Home means many things to many people. But there are some common factors in what we want home to be. Unconditional love. Comfort. Acceptance. Safety. Rest. Most us would agree that home should embody these things.

Some of us can still visit our childhood homes; some cannot. Some of us still have the "homefolks," our parents, but they may be residents in a facility that is not the home we love. Others have no desire to visit home because it is an unwelcoming, unfriendly, and undesirable place. Regardless, I believe all of us have an image in our hearts of what home should be. And this is what pulls at us when we talk about heaven. After all, heaven is home. Really. It will have all the attributes and amenities we instinctively crave.

Jesus told those gathered around Him that day that He was going to prepare a place to welcome all those in relationship with Him. It will be a place for God's family to be together forever. There will be no lack of love or comfort. There will be perfect peace, harmony, and rest. No family member will be sick or waiting for test results or unable to join in the festivities. There will be room for everybody, and the joy will be eternal.

Your earthly home may not be the place you want to go, but heaven will fulfill all your dreams. Hold on to that promise. You can go home!

FATHER IN HEAVEN, I WANT TO LIVE IN YOUR HOME FOR
ETERNITY. THANK YOU FOR MAKING A WAY FOR ME TO GO THERE
THROUGH YOUR SON, JESUS. HOLD MY SPOT OPEN! AMEN.

DREAM

AND NOW, LORD, WHAT WAIT I FOR? MY HOPE IS IN THEE.
Psalm 39:7

It's irritating not to be able to remember the dream you had last night. Haven't you experienced this? You wake up with the emotion fresh upon you from your traumatic or hilarious night adventure and are sure you'll remember it so you can relate it to family and coworkers. But you don't. And when you try to describe it, it's a jumble of vague images and feelings.

There were many people in Bible times who had dreams. And believe me, they were so vivid that recalling them was not a problem! Before humans had His Word and His Spirit on earth, God often spoke to them through dreams. It seems that this is a rarer phenomenon today, although in some areas of the world where His written revelation is difficult to obtain, it is happening frequently.

Dreams may be significant or not. Usually, they are the result of our minds taking events from the day before and worries about the day ahead and creating a story out of them. And what stories! Probably it's a good thing we can't remember them all. We might doubt our own sanity if we could.

But there is another type of dream as well. These are the dreams we have for the future—plans, hopes, and expectations. If they come from God or are born out of our surrender to Him, they are good. If they arise from our own ambition, they may not be. The Bible records examples of both.

What are your dreams for the future? Have you considered God in them? Are you waiting for the fulfillment of a God-given dream? Continue to take the next step and watch as He leads the way. If He can make the dreams of Joseph come true, with all the delays and detours, He can do the same for you.

LORD, MY DREAMS AND MY HOPES AND MY FUTURE ARE IN YOUR HANDS. LEAD ME IN THE NEXT STEP AS I WAIT ON YOU. AMEN.

IT WAS MEET THAT WE SHOULD MAKE MERRY,
AND BE GLAD: FOR THIS THY BROTHER WAS DEAD, AND
IS ALIVE AGAIN; AND WAS LOST, AND IS FOUND.
Luke 15:32

Party hats.

Balloons.

Crepe paper streamers.

Kazoos.

Cake.

Punch.

Cheers.

Do you like celebrations? My family always made a big deal out of birthdays. We didn't always have a big, flashy party with outside guests and expensive gifts, but we did have a cake of some kind, candles, a few thoughtful gifts, and lots of congratulating and love. My mother was of the opinion that special days deserved special ceremony.

I think God is like that. In fact, we get our love of celebration from Him. He made us, after all. He makes a big deal out of the number of hairs on our heads and the tragic fall of a bird from a branch. He instituted the feast days and the holy days. He believes in celebration.

Today's verse, taken from the account of the Prodigal Son in the Gospel of Luke, informs us that God especially celebrates when any one of us receives His gift of salvation. He is ecstatic about the lost being found. There is no greater joy for a parent than the restoration of a child. And that is only a glimpse of how God feels when one of His creation comes back into relationship with Him.

Your family of origin may not have even recognized birthdays or holidays, but when you join God's forever family, you sign up for celebrations of every kind. And they will continue for eternity!

LORD, THANK YOU FOR RECEIVING ME INTO
YOUR FAMILY THROUGH YOUR SON, JESUS. TODAY I
CELEBRATE MY RELATIONSHIP WITH YOU. AMEN.

BUT THOU. . .FOLLOW AFTER RIGHTEOUSNESS,
GODLINESS, FAITH, LOVE, PATIENCE, MEEKNESS.
1 Timothy 6:11

If life is a journey, then perseverance is the fuel that keeps us going. The apostle Paul certainly knew about perseverance. When he wrote these words to the young pastor, Timothy, he wasn't giving hollow advice. He had lived it.

Living a Christian life requires effort. God will not take action for us that we can take ourselves. He did what we cannot do—He provided the means of atonement. But He expects us to do what we can do—make daily choices for good. The word Paul used in this verse is *follow*. It suggests actively taking steps in the path of another. One has to purposely follow; it does not happen by accident.

Perseverance is really the theme of John Bunyan's classic novel, *The Pilgrim's Progress*. The pilgrim, or Christian as he is later called, begins his journey at the cross by accepting God's gift of forgiveness, but he must continue along the path toward the Celestial City, making daily progress, fighting spiritual battles, and winning victory over self. God did not have in mind that we should be babies, carried along the path toward heaven. Rather, He calls us to be warriors, standing in His strength as we go through this life.

In another of his epistles, Paul wrote under the inspiration of the Spirit about the spiritual armor we must put on so that we can be victorious in our Christian lives. When we are properly clothed in the protection God provides, we can face with assurance whatever comes.

The concept of perseverance in faith and commitment is seen throughout the Bible. And it is a trait we must adopt so that we too can make our own progress toward the City.

HEAVENLY FATHER, I KNOW I CAN'T LIVE VICTORIOUSLY IN MY OWN STRENGTH, BUT I CAN IN YOURS. PUT OTHERS IN MY LIFE TO REMIND ME NOT TO GIVE UP AND HELP ME KEEP ON, DAY BY DAY. IN JESUS' NAME, AMEN.

BUT LAY UP FOR YOURSELVES TREASURES IN HEAVEN,
WHERE NEITHER MOTH NOR RUST DOTH CORRUPT, AND
WHERE THIEVES DO NOT BREAK THROUGH NOR STEAL.
Matthew 6:20

Treasure—it's a word we don't use much today. Treasure makes us think of pirates and ancient secrets and sunken ships. When we speak of our valuables in the twenty-first century, it's usually in terms of assets and IRAs and retirement funds. But it means the same thing as the word Jesus used. It refers to our carefully hoarded pile.

And God's Word admonishes us to be wise and to prepare for the future. We are not to be slothful and lazy. Yet Jesus told those listening to Him that day long ago that they should not stockpile earthly stuff. What's the difference?

Jesus always went for the intent of the heart in His teaching. And He was speaking not only to poverty-stricken Jews under Roman rule but also to us today. The message is the same. Don't dream about your bank account; dream about heaven's riches. Earthly money loses value. Gold may be lost and never recovered. Thieves are around to steal whatever they can find. What we save on this earth is temporary. But when we store up riches in heaven, we are saving them to the cloud, to use modern language. They are untouchable, safe, reserved in perfect condition.

How do we store up treasure in heaven? We do it by valuing godliness above success, by choosing a God-honoring church over moving to a new job without one, by going to worship on Sunday rather than working, by giving our resources to missions instead of buying a second home or a new boat or an additional vehicle. There are many ways in which we can make the choice to value the eternal above the temporal. And every time we do, our heavenly fund grows beautifully, not only for us but for the benefit of others as well.

GOD, MY FATHER, I WANT TO INVEST IN WHAT REALLY MATTERS. MY ABILITIES AND MY RESOURCES AND MY ENERGIES ARE YOURS. AMEN.

WHATSOEVER THINGS ARE TRUE, WHATSOEVER THINGS ARE
HONEST, WHATSOEVER THINGS ARE JUST, WHATSOEVER THINGS
ARE PURE, WHATSOEVER THINGS ARE LOVELY, WHATSOEVER
THINGS ARE OF GOOD REPORT; IF THERE BE ANY VIRTUE,
AND IF THERE BE ANY PRAISE, THINK ON THESE THINGS.
Philippians 4:8

Memories smell like cedar to me. When I was little, my grandmother would let me
carefully rummage through my late aunt's cedar chest. It was a large hope chest, filled
to the brim with all the memorabilia of her short life. Dying of kidney failure at age
twenty-seven, my aunt entered heaven before I came into this world. I never knew
her. But what she liked and what she collected were alive to me in that chest—dolls
and fabric and teacups and collectible spoons and cards and pictures and handmade
crafts, all scented with cedar.

In the pictures, she smiled at me, loving life, a little saucy but with a demure attitude. The family remembered her love of music and Jesus, her manner, and her tragic early death. Mostly, they recalled the true and honest things, the pure and lovely and virtuous traits she possessed.

It has long been considered bad manners to speak ill of the dead. While it is true that the deceased may have been a scoundrel, those of good breeding understand that some things are best forgotten when the culprit lies cold in the graveyard. One should remark on the kind and generous activities of those gone, and if they be few, there will be less of which to speak.

One day, it will be us on the other side of the conversation. The funeral parlor lights will cast their pinkish tinge over the casket, the flowers' aroma will pervade the environment, and the preacher will stand beside the family to receive condolences. Let's give our loved ones a file folder of good things to say. Let's help them with their memories so that remembering something praiseworthy doesn't tax their mental faculties. Whether you have a cedar chest or not, they will be so grateful.

LORD, ENABLE ME TO LIVE A LIFE THAT HELPS OTHERS FOCUS ON WHAT IS GODLY AND GOOD. LET MY LIFE BE A LIVING TESTIMONY, WHETHER I'M ALIVE ON THIS EARTH OR IN HEAVEN WITH YOU. AMEN.

NOW UNTO HIM THAT IS ABLE TO DO EXCEEDING ABUNDANTLY
ABOVE ALL THAT WE ASK OR THINK, ACCORDING TO THE POWER
THAT WORKETH IN US, UNTO HIM BE GLORY IN THE CHURCH BY
CHRIST JESUS THROUGHOUT ALL AGES, WORLD WITHOUT END. AMEN.

Ephesians 3:20–21

We have a new church in our community. It's called Imagine Church. I don't know what they teach. I haven't studied their basic doctrine. I don't even know if they're biblical. But I assume that they take their name from a desire to see what God will do if they attempt great things in His name.

William Carey, missionary trailblazer of years past, first voiced this idea: "Attempt great things for God; expect great things from God." I think he's on to something. God will not be boxed in by what we think is possible or doable. He will not be limited by our funds or resources or personalities or abilities. His work can be thwarted only by our lack of faith.

Imagination is highly touted in raising today's child. Parents are advised to encourage little ones to imagine and create. Experts recognize that allowing the mind to wander not only stretches one's ability to think but also promotes intelligence by giving the younger generation the hope that they can accomplish great things. Those who do not imagine do not do.

God tells us in these verses from the letter to the Ephesians that He wants us to imagine great things in His name. We are not to seek our own glory, of course, but He wants us to dream of holy adventure, to plot and plan how we can do what hasn't yet been done for Him. In the 1950s in Ecuador, five missionary men and their wives schemed about how to reach an isolated jungle tribe. Their imagination came to fruition, and though it led to the young men's martyrdom, it resulted in the complete transformation of that people group and in the calling of thousands of other young men and women into ministry and missions. That's definitely more than any of them asked or thought.

....
....
....
....
....
....
....
....
....
....
....

LORD JESUS, PLANT IN MY HEART AND MIND THE SEEDS OF
WHAT YOU WANT ME TO DREAM FOR YOU. LET ME IMAGINE
AND THEN DO GREAT THINGS FOR YOUR KINGDOM. AMEN.

UNIQUE

I WILL PRAISE THEE; FOR I AM FEARFULLY AND
WONDERFULLY MADE: MARVELLOUS ARE THY WORKS;
AND THAT MY SOUL KNOWETH RIGHT WELL.
Psalm 139:14

You are unique just by being born. There is no other human with your exact DNA, fingerprints, or personality.

Perhaps this is one of the greatest philosophical arguments against abortion. When a child is aborted, the world loses something (someone) that can never be replaced. In a culture that values individuality, this is tragic on so many levels.

God, the incredible Genius behind everything we know, planned that every human being would be irreplaceable. Just as He crafts the inimitable design of every snowflake, He pours His image in a unique way into every male or female conceived on this earth. There, in embryonic form, is the blueprint of an amazing and one-of-a-kind life.

Before the days of sonograms and digital imaging, the psalmist was given insight into the knowledge of our Creator, who sees every cell as it is formed and knows us from the chromosomal level and even deeper. David, writing in ancient times, called this marvelous. And so it is.

No scan of the body, analysis of the mind, or confession of the heart can let others know us the way He does. And for the billions of humans now living and the billions who have gone before, He has the same intimate knowledge.

Satan, the enemy of God, doesn't want you to think about this. He wants you to lose sight of your uniqueness amid the masses of people on the face of the earth. But Satan is a liar and deceiver. Refuse his lies. Hold to what is true. Your Creator made you distinctively, He knows you intimately, and He loves you completely. Develop your relationship with Him today.

GOD, THERE IS NO ONE LIKE ME. AND YOU WANTED THERE
TO BE A ME. SO RIGHT NOW, I ASK YOU TO TAKE ME AND
FILL ME AND USE ME AND CHANGE ME ON THE INSIDE
UNTIL I REFLECT YOUR GLORY. IN JESUS' NAME, AMEN.

LOYAL

AND WHATSOEVER YE DO, DO IT HEARTILY,
AS TO THE LORD, AND NOT UNTO MEN.
Colossians 3:23

Loyalty cards are common in retail. Your keychain probably holds many of them. They help you get the best prices where you shop. Scan the card when you check out and get a better deal. But alas, loyalty in consumers is not very deep. They can be swayed to another store by cheaper prices. You're probably the same way.

Retailers of yesteryear didn't worry as much about consumer loyalty. When entrepreneurs like Sears, Roebuck and Company; J. C. Penney; and F. W. Woolworth were establishing their stores, they built them on stellar customer service and product guarantee. The American public was dazzled by the treatment they received and threw their shopping trade into the ring of their favorite. Relationship was ultimately more important than pricing to many.

God wants us to be loyal in our work for Him. It isn't about the recognition or success; it's about doing the best job with committed hearts.

When we serve or minister with our good in mind, we are not giving Him, the God of the universe, the loyalty He deserves. We are like the fickle shopper, lured by whoever offers a few cents' savings this week. But when we do our work heartily, with gusto and passion, as though we are actually on the job with God as our supervisor, we are showing loyalty of spirit.

....

....

....

....

GOD, HELP ME TODAY TO WORK HEARTILY FOR YOU
AND NOT FOR THE GLORY OF ANYONE ELSE. I WANT MY
LOYALTY TO YOUR KINGDOM TO BE STEADFAST. AMEN.

IN THE FEAR OF THE Lord IS STRONG CONFIDENCE.
Proverbs 14:26

Most beauty products promise an aura of confidence. While it is not exclusively a feminine malady, many women struggle with confidence as it relates to their appearance. Women know instinctively that they are made to be beauty bearers; yet because of the assault of sin on the genetic code, most of us cannot claim real beauty. Our culture assures us that if we are truly being the women we should be, we will be attractive and confident as the eyes of everyone we meet assess us. And of course, the beauty product being advertised will help with that!

Men also struggle with confidence, but it seems to be more strongly tied to their abilities than to their looks, though there is probably some of that as well. Whatever the cause, across the human spectrum, we often lack confidence and despise ourselves for it.

The writer of Proverbs reminds us that true confidence is found in the Lord of heaven. That is the only source where we can gain the assurance we need. We don't have what it takes. That is a fact. But He does. And we don't have to rely on our appearance or our abilities or whatever to give us the boost for today.

We can be confident if we have a reverence (fear) of the Lord. We honor Him in His rightful place if we surrender ourselves to His purpose and if we trust in His power to accomplish what needs to be done. This is the aura of confidence that can only come from Him.

LORD, I NEED CONFIDENCE. YOUR WORD SAYS THAT I CAN HAVE IT IF I CULTIVATE A REVERENCE FOR YOU. I SURRENDER MYSELF TO YOU TODAY. IN JESUS' NAME, AMEN.

Healing

AND JESUS WENT ABOUT ALL THE CITIES AND VILLAGES,
TEACHING IN THEIR SYNAGOGUES, AND PREACHING
THE GOSPEL OF THE KINGDOM, AND HEALING EVERY
SICKNESS AND EVERY DISEASE AMONG THE PEOPLE.
Matthew 9:35

Essential oils.

Aromatherapy.

Whole foods.

Holistic healing.

We are concerned with healthy living today. And many of these approaches have merit. From ancient times, the human family recognized the need to use herbs and potions and medicines to alleviate pain and cure disease.

The Old Testament records the struggle of God's people with illness and death. Leprosy was a malady that brought great suffering and ended in isolation and untimely demise. Remember the story of how a servant girl told Naaman's wife about the prophet's healing powers? Have you read the Levitical laws and the rules and regulations that the Israelites were supposed to observe regarding certain diseases and conditions? With hardly any resources and no modern medical advances, there was little hope for the common person who encountered a life-threatening condition.

The Gospels tell story after story of how Jesus went to the cities and villages of His day, not only teaching and preaching but also healing. What a wonder that must have been! The evangelist preaches *and* heals. For Jesus, the ability to bring relief from suffering must have been a joy. For Him to take away the effects of sin's curse, even for a little while, surely brought Him holy delight.

We are admonished in scripture to pray for healing when we are sick, and most of us do ask our friends and family and church congregations to pray when a health tragedy strikes. But there are times when God chooses to heal in heaven. And that is just as surely an answer as earthly healing, for only He can give eternal, pain-free life to us all.

LORD, YOU ARE THE GREAT PHYSICIAN. THANK YOU FOR YOUR POWER TO HEAL. I TRUST YOU WITH MY HEALTH TODAY. AMEN.

AND WE KNOW THAT ALL THINGS WORK TOGETHER
FOR GOOD TO THEM THAT LOVE GOD, TO THEM WHO
ARE THE CALLED ACCORDING TO HIS PURPOSE.

Romans 8:28

The purpose of God is what is right and good. We were made to be part of it. Perhaps you have heard the statement that God is more concerned with us being holy than with us being happy. It is a philosophical and theological pond in which it is fun to swim. But I wonder if, truthfully, they are one and the same. God knows that, unless we are holy, we will not be happy. And if we are truly happy, it is because we are holy.

Holy does not mean stodgy and aloof. Holy means totally good, like Jesus. That is complete happiness because we were made to be in harmony with Him, and without that component, we cannot know true fulfillment.

When we are aligned with His purpose, we know that He is working out all things for our good. This doesn't mean that every single happening *is* good, but that it is part of the plan accomplishing His ultimate good in our world and for His kingdom. With that purpose in mind, you and I can rest in His ability to coordinate all the loose ends and seemingly random events into a logical and beautiful pattern for eternity.

The proof of the recipe is the finished result of combining the ingredients. The desired garment is what appears when all the pieces of fabric have been assembled. The longed-for grade happens when every assignment and test has been averaged. And the victorious and eternal purpose of God will someday be fulfilled when all the bits of earthly time have been assimilated into His holy plan.

GOD, YOU ARE WORKING OUT YOUR PERFECT AND COMPLETE AND ETERNAL PLAN. I TRUST MY PART IN IT TO YOUR PURPOSE. AMEN.

WITH MEN THIS IS IMPOSSIBLE; BUT WITH
GOD ALL THINGS ARE POSSIBLE.
Matthew 19:26

If you believed that anything you attempted for God was possible, what would you do? Go on a mission trip? Start a new ministry? Get a different job? Apply for Bible college? Teach a Sunday School class? Volunteer in the bus ministry?

Guess what? Anything you attempt for God *is* possible. Jesus said it. With God, *all* things are possible.

Do we need to seek counsel at times? Yes. Do we need to pray about it? Sure. But should we let fear stop us if God seems to be opening the doors? No.

Think about the impossible happenings in scripture:

A man building a boat that withstood a worldwide flood.

A ninety-year-old woman giving birth.

A shepherd boy killing a giant warrior.

A fisherman preaching to thousands.

A roomful of followers upsetting the known world.

God specializes in the impossible. When man stamps the word *impossible* on the next event at hand, God smiles and makes it happen.

Many of the great heroes of faith whose biographies we read did not let the word *impossible* deter them. Think about George Müller, who opened orphanages in England and ran them without asking for a penny of support. How about D. L. Moody, a shoe salesman in Chicago who was used by God to lead thousands to Christ and establish a Bible college that exists to this day? There was Billy Sunday, the professional baseball player turned preacher. There was Gladys Aylward, the English parlor maid who went to China with barely any money and no training, and Amy Carmichael, who rescued hundreds of girls from the temple brothels in India. None of them let the impossibilities looming ahead stop them. And neither should we.

LORD, THERE IS NO IMPOSSIBILITY IN YOUR WORLD, ONLY POSSIBILITIES THAT YOU CAN BRING TO PASS. HELP ME NEVER TO BE AFRAID TO ATTEMPT WHAT YOU SHOW ME TO DO. AMEN.

FOR MY YOKE IS EASY, AND MY BURDEN IS LIGHT.
Matthew 11:30

A few years back, the word *simplify* was a common theme in country decorating. Wooden signs were painted with it, and it was a chant for many who wanted a return to the days of primitive stylings. I think this desire is the reason for the popularity of observing Amish life, both in travel and in novels. The appeal of the simple life is intoxicating. With our high-speed internet and our expressways, our fast-food meals and K-Cup coffee, we are continually in the fast lane of life. The idea of slowing down and getting rid of many of the extra weights of living has a magical allure.

Earthly life is not simple. It is filled with busyness and noise, with hustle and bustle, with many things that clamor for our attention. And those who live in the secluded country cannot escape all of the tangles of modern life either. Even those who cloister themselves away in monasteries or convents often further seclude themselves in cells under a vow of silence, trying to elude their own thoughts and words.

God knows that our distractions are many and our struggles weigh us down. In Jesus, He beckons us to the simple life of the soul. Lean on Him for strength.

Now, we have to admit that the Christian life is not void of struggle. In fact, it may have more struggle than that of a non-Christian because Satan fights hard against anyone who identifies with Christ. So the life God offers us is not *easy*, but it is *simple*. And those who discover the secret of taking to Him all the concerns of life can rest a little easier, without becoming Amish or living in a monastery.

FATHER GOD, THE SECRET OF SIMPLE TRUST IS ONE I WANT
TO LEARN WELL. HELP ME TO KEEP FROM STRUGGLING
AND TO BRING ALL MY CONCERNS TO YOU. AMEN.

EVERY MAN ACCORDING AS HE PURPOSETH IN HIS
HEART, SO LET HIM GIVE; NOT GRUDGINGLY, OR OF
NECESSITY: FOR GOD LOVETH A CHEERFUL GIVER.
2 Corinthians 9:7

Who could have guessed that one of our all-time favorite stories would be about a miser? You guessed it! *A Christmas Carol.*

Charles Dickens was on point with that little tale, though I'm sure he didn't realize at the time how wildly popular it would become decades after his death. I believe the thread of redemption that runs through the story appeals to something deep inside us. We love the idea that a grouch can become a grandpa figure, a tightwad can become a benefactor.

God loves generosity too. It is a trait that He embodies. He was generous beyond our wildest imaginations when He sent His Son to be our replacement on the cross.

He is generous in His grace to us every day. He is generous in the provisions of light and breath and health. And He is generous in His promise of heaven.

When we belong to Him, the Holy Spirit is at work to develop His nature in us. He wants us to reflect His goodness and holiness, and generosity is one of those attributes. Our Father is delighted when we cooperate with His adjustments in our temperament. He is thrilled when He sees us share a generous attitude.

Scrooge became a giver after he was confronted with his evil nature on Christmas Eve with four ghostly encounters. We can become givers after an encounter with the God of the universe, the One who has given and continues to give more than any of us could hope for. We can give money, time, friendship, affirmation, love, and assistance. Don't clutch your measly resources to yourself. Open up your store house and share what God has given you. And you'll have more than enough for yourself.

....

....

....

....

....

....

....

....

....

....

....

GOD, THANK YOU FOR GIVING ME EVERYTHING I NEED TO
LIVE IN RELATIONSHIP WITH YOU. DEVELOP A SPIRIT OF
GENEROSITY IN ME SO THAT I CAN BE MORE LIKE YOU. AMEN.

WHY ART THOU CAST DOWN, O MY SOUL? AND WHY ART THOU DISQUIETED WITHIN ME? HOPE THOU IN GOD: FOR I SHALL YET PRAISE HIM, WHO IS THE HEALTH OF MY COUNTENANCE, AND MY GOD.

Psalm 42:11

Optimists are often accused of ignoring reality. But those who know the Lord should have an upward look and a hopeful spirit.

While it is okay to acknowledge and be concerned over the ravages of sin in the world, it is not right for believers to dwell on gloom and doom. The life of God within us gives us the buoyancy to look ahead to a future totally kept by His mighty hand. A little poem by an unknown author gives us a lighthearted look at what an optimistic attitude can be:

The Cork and the Whale

A little brown cork
Fell in the path of a whale
Who lashed it down
With his angry tail.
But, in spite of the blows,
It quickly arose,
And floated serenely
Before his nose.
Said the cork to the whale,
"You may flap and sputter and frown,
But you never, never can keep me down:
For I'm made of the stuff
That is buoyant enough
To float instead of to drown."

You are going to be slapped around today by the waves of life. And Satan will see to it that thoughts of giving up in despair float into your mind. Resist his lies. Say no to gloom. Hope in God, and don't let your soul be cast down!

....
....
....
....
....
....
....
....

LORD, I KNOW ALL MY HOPE IS FOUND IN YOU. GIVE ME AN OPTIMISTIC SPIRIT BASED ON THE PROMISE THAT YOU ARE IN CONTROL. AMEN.

EVERY DEVOTED THING IS MOST HOLY UNTO THE LORD.
Leviticus 27:28

Sports figures are paid the big bucks. What they rake in for kicking, dribbling, hitting, and throwing various kinds of athletic balls is more than many public officials and emergency medical technicians make and certainly exceeds the salaries of missionaries and pastors. They are paid to entertain us, not to help us be better citizens or save our lives or our souls. While athletics has its place in our lives, it seems the American public today simply has put a premium on their sports stars.

The one thing we must acknowledge though is their devotion to their game. Many of them begin at very early ages and spend hour after hour in the gym, on the field, on the court, or on the green. They completely consecrate themselves to the sport. And it shows in their game.

God asks us to be wholly devoted, consecrated to Him. In the Old Testament, objects used in tabernacle worship had to go through a ceremony of cleansing and consecration. So did the priests who performed the holy rites. In the New Testament, God inspired the human writers to call us to consecration of ourselves as the living "temples" of the Holy Spirit. We are to be set apart for His use.

The Bible knows nothing of tainted vessels used for God. Everything He used to accomplish His Work was purified and sanctified. He still uses that process today when it comes to people. Through the blood of Christ, we can be washed and set apart for His use. We can be wholly devoted *to* and made holy *for* the Lord.

JEHOVAH GOD, CLEANSE ME AND SANCTIFY ME. SET ME APART FOR YOUR SERVICE. LET ME BE YOUR VESSEL. IN JESUS' NAME, AMEN.

Who doesn't love dipping her head to receive a medal? Whether it's awards night at the end of the school year or the finish line of a marathon, the one who does the work rejoices in the reward.

God is into rewards. He never loses sight of the work done or misplaces the file of the faithful. He abundantly and plentifully rewards them.

He also reserves appropriate consequences for those who disdain His laws and spurn His grace. The Bible tells us that vengeance belongs to Him alone. While He is merciful and not willing that any human being be separated from Him for eternity, He is also just and fair. Those who choose life apart from Him will be granted the reward of that choice—eternal death.

The Bible does not encourage us to be reward focused, but it does inspire us with the thought of a crown of life and the words from our Lord: *"Well done, good and faithful servant."* Many of God's servants are not granted commendation or recognition in this life. The rewards for their labors in pulpits and on foreign fields, their suffering in prisons and work camps, and their witnessing in big and small ways are delayed but not denied. There is coming a day of reckoning when everything will be brought into account, and those who have served will be rewarded. Plan to be in the group of the faithful.

LORD, I'M GLAD YOU KEEP PERFECT ACCOUNTS. I DON'T HAVE
TO WORRY ABOUT YOUR RECORDS OR WORRY ABOUT YOUR
HARDWORKING SERVANTS. THE REWARDS ARE COMING. AMEN.

BUT THOU, O LORD, ART A GOD FULL OF COMPASSION, AND
GRACIOUS, LONG SUFFERING, AND PLENTEOUS IN MERCY AND TRUTH.
Psalm 86:15

In every caring nurse and doctor, we can glimpse the image of God. Without Him, compassion does not exist. With Him, it is present in abundance.

You can test your level of compassion by going to emergency departments, mental hospitals, nursing homes, and prisons. In these halls are the most easily disregarded or dehumanized people. Some can do nothing to help themselves. Others don't want to. Some had no choice in their condition; others deliberately chose a wrong path which led there. Those who work in these institutions may or may not feel compassion toward their charges. Admittedly, it is difficult to feel kindly toward those who snub their noses at society. And even for those who are disabled through no fault of their own, the discomfort we feel for abnormality and deformity must be overcome if we are to experience a sense of compassion.

God, the psalmist says, is full of compassion. There is no lack of kindly feeling in Him, though He is perfect in every way, holy and completely pure. He sees the imperfection and filth of our world, the piteous condition of broken humankind, and He does not recoil. Rather, He points the way to His Son, who came to touch blinded eyes and withered hands and twisted bodies and tortured minds and, most importantly, sin-ravaged souls. Jesus did not draw back from the most undesirable. He sought them out. He loved them. He healed them. This is the message of compassion in His Word.

_____

_____

_____

_____

_____

_____

_____

_____

_____

_____

_____

_____

_____

_____

_____

FATHER GOD, THANK YOU FOR BEING FILLED WITH COMPASSION. CREATE IN ME A SPIRIT OF KINDNESS TOWARD THOSE LESS FORTUNATE AND THOSE RAVAGED BY SIN. IN JESUS' NAME, AMEN.

Fruitful

THAT YE MIGHT WALK WORTHY OF THE LORD UNTO
ALL PLEASING, BEING FRUITFUL IN EVERY GOOD WORK,
AND INCREASING IN THE KNOWLEDGE OF GOD.
Colossians 1:10

The hope of every gardener is that the harvest will be plentiful. That's another word for fruitful.

In scripture, our relationship with the Lord is often compared with the process of growth in nature. Because it is observable in every place and in every generation, God knew that most readers would readily see the similarities.

Fruitfulness is a sign of health in plants. It is the optimal state. The tiny green shoots ingest the sunlight and rain, endure pruning of leaves, sink roots down deep, and one day produce blossoms and then full fruit, whether blooms, fruits, or vegetables.

Jesus taught His followers that they must stay connected to Him as the Source, the Vine, in order to stay healthy and grow. He said that, at times, the gardener had to prune plants that were not doing well so that they could bear fruit. He also warned that plants that refused to bear fruit of any kind were in danger of being disconnected from the source altogether.

Every follower of Christ will bear fruit at some time in some way. It is impossible to be connected to the Source and not be fruitful. In the verse for today, Paul told the Colossian believers that they should be fruitful in every good work. There is no loophole. We are called to show the life within us by the fruit visible on us.

LORD JESUS, I WANT TO BEAR FRUIT IN YOUR NAME. PRUNE ME WHEN I NEED IT, AND FEED ME ON YOUR WORD AS MY SOURCE OF LIFE. AMEN.

Harvest is the season of abundance. Images of wagons filled with pumpkins, fields dotted with hay bales, and baskets of shiny apples tease our minds every fall as we think of the bounty with which we are blessed. Harvest is a time of rich color and hard work and many blessings. It reminds us of the gracious goodness of God.

In ancient times, abundance was scarcer. There were no modern conveniences. Growing things took more work and energy. There was no way to predict weather patterns or irrigate fields or store up the produce by canning or freezing. When times of abundance did come, it was met with great joy and thanksgiving.

False religions in other cultures often attribute either abundance or famine to the whim of their gods. They believe they must pacify their deities so that their families may have enough to eat. And they believe they must give them gifts in order to assure their peace in the afterlife.

The truth of the one true God is that He is abundant in goodness and truth, and He provides what we need to live for Him in every season of life. The Bible tells us that He gives food to the creatures in the woods and on the plains. He causes the rain to fall and the sun to shine and the food to grow. Whatever abundance we have is because of Him.

....
....
....
....
....
....
....
....
....
....
....
....
....
....
....
....
....
....

HEAVENLY FATHER, YOU ARE THE ABUNDANT GOD, THE GIVER AND SUSTAINER OF LIFE. THANK YOU FOR IT ALL. AMEN.

GLORY YE IN HIS HOLY NAME: LET THE HEART
OF THEM REJOICE THAT SEEK THE Lord.
1 Chronicles 16:10

It's a word I commonly associate with Christmas music. *Rejoice.* It seems to call for bells and chimes and carols. We don't do much rejoicing today. Well, at least we don't call it that. But we do the same thing in our texts with our emojis. Our keyboards have a range of faces from which to choose, from apple-cheeked smirks to toothy grins to tear-dripping laughs. We use them to "rejoice" in our conversations with friends and family.

I have become so accustomed to using my friendly emojis that a texting conversation seems awkward and rude without them. They help to ease bold statements and make happy news even brighter. While I have drawn smiley faces in my correspondence in times past, I have never seen them as almost part of the words themselves until recently.

Today's verse instructs us to let our hearts rejoice in the Lord. This is more than clicking a smiley face on the screen of life. It is a deep acknowledgment of the sovereign oversight of our God. It is a leaning on His wisdom. It is a trust in His Word.

How can you rejoice in Him today?

Thank Him for salvation.

Look for a new blessing.

Remember answers to prayer.

Look forward to heaven.

....

....

....

....

....

....

....

....

....

....

....

....

....

....

....

FATHER, I WANT TO REJOICE IN YOU TODAY. THANK YOU
FOR GIVING ME SO MANY THINGS TO PRACTICE ON. AMEN.

TRUST IN HIM AT ALL TIMES; YE PEOPLE, POUR OUT YOUR
HEART BEFORE HIM: GOD IS A REFUGE FOR US.
Psalm 62:8

I like historical sites. When I was small, my family would visit famous places when we were near them. From battlefields to colonial homes, we oohed and aahed over the bricks and mortar, the trinkets and clothing.

I remember being intrigued by the forts. These primitive blockades were often erected in the early American wilderness to protect the settlers from native attacks. They were usually constructed of logs with guard towers on the corners and gates at the entrance. They were often outfitted with holes for the weapons and with fortified rooms inside for more protection. They were places of refuge.

David, the writer of many psalms, understood the need for refuge. As a young man, he had to flee into the wilderness to escape the mad jealousy of King Saul. He often lived in caves, taking refuge in the barren places of the earth. When he penned these words about trusting in God at all times, he was speaking out of the depth of his own experience. Jehovah had been a Refuge for his soul in very dark times.

God does not want us to escape reality, but He does offer us a sanctuary in His presence, a place of calm in which to rest and fortify ourselves for the next advance. He has promised to cover us with His hand of protection and give us strength.

....

....

....

....

....

....

....

....

....

....

....

....

....

....

....

....

ALMIGHTY GOD, THERE IS NO REFUGE LIKE YOU.
I NEED YOUR PROTECTION AND STRENGTH IN THIS
WILDERNESS I'M FACING. IN JESUS' NAME, AMEN.

WORTHY IS THE LAMB THAT WAS SLAIN TO RECEIVE
POWER, AND RICHES, AND WISDOM, AND STRENGTH,
AND HONOUR, AND GLORY, AND BLESSING.
Revelation 5:12

Worthy is a word similar to *deserve*. Both of them should be used sparingly. I rarely buy a greeting card that uses the word *deserve*. To me, birthdays and anniversaries aren't about deserving. None of us deserve good things simply by being alive. No, we are granted these blessings by a gracious God.

And the word *worthy* has a similar connotation, suggesting that the recipient merits the praise being given.

The only One truly deserving and worthy of praise and glory is He whom the Father has set at His right hand, the Lamb slain from the foundation of the world, Jesus Christ.

The word *deserve* may appropriately be used in at least one very important reference. Those who serve our country and its citizens and put their lives in danger to do so are certainly deserving of honor and recognition. Those in the armed forces, firefighters, and law enforcement officers are all very worthy of our esteem. They are risking their lives to help others.

This is what Jesus did for us on a much grander scale. He not only risked His life, He laid it down of His own free will and became a sacrifice for us all. Because of this, God has exalted Him and given Him a name above all others. There is no name in heaven or on the earth that is more worthy of worship than His.

LORD GOD, I HONOR THE NAME OF JESUS TODAY.
HE IS WORTHY OF ALL MY PRAISE AND THANKS. I BOW
MY HEAD AND HEART TO HIM RIGHT NOW. AMEN.

THESE THINGS I HAVE SPOKEN UNTO YOU, THAT IN ME YE
MIGHT HAVE PEACE. IN THE WORLD YE SHALL HAVE TRIBULATION:
BUT BE OF GOOD CHEER; I HAVE OVERCOME THE WORLD.

John 16:33

Some battles are harder to fight alone. The founder of Weight Watchers hit upon a winning concept in the idea of group support. There is strength in numbers, and when those who have similar struggles come together to cheer on one another and celebrate the successes, victory is more likely to occur. Those who enter the Weight Watchers program are set on overcoming their indulgence for food. It is impossible, of course, to overcome the desire for food. At least it is in healthy individuals. The craving for nourishment is what keeps us alive. But it is possible to hold that desire in moderation, to keep in check the irrational and uncontrollable desire to consume large quantities of unnecessary calories.

Jesus told us that we can be overcomers. We don't have to be defeated by temptation to sin. We don't have to give in to undisciplined appetites. We don't have to be held hostage by intemperance. We can triumph over them because of His grace. He even designed a support system for us. It's called the church, the body of believers who meet together on a regular basis to encourage one another and cheer for one another, to pray for each other and hold each other accountable. This group meeting is vital for success. The Christian life is not meant to be a solo event.

Whatever you're facing today, you can have victory if you lean on Him and trust your support system. Don't try to go it alone. Determine to overcome.

LORD, YOU DESIGNED A PLAN FOR ME TO BE AN OVERCOMER.
I PLAN TO TAKE ADVANTAGE OF EVERYTHING YOU OFFER ME
SO THAT I CAN HAVE VICTORY. IN JESUS' NAME, AMEN.

LIGHT

I AM THE LIGHT OF THE WORLD: HE THAT FOLLOWETH ME SHALL NOT WALK IN DARKNESS, BUT SHALL HAVE THE LIGHT OF LIFE.

John 8:12

I like night-lights. I always have. Some crave pitch darkness. But I had enough of that in a damp cave when the electric lights were switched off, and we were told to put a hand in front of our faces. Nothing. No shadows, no trace of anything, total black. No, thank you. And I prefer a night-light on somewhere nearby so I can see at least the outlines of my room.

Darkness is disorienting. In darkness, there is no sense of direction or balance. It is impossible to avoid bumping into things. Those who are physically blind learn to successfully navigate what would challenge people with sight. Darkness and loss of vision go together.

The Old Testament prophet Isaiah wrote that before Christ the people were in great darkness. And there is even a period of time after Christ that is called the Dark Ages because of the absence of illumination through God's revelation.

Jesus came to bring the light. In fact, He is the Light, the very source from which all other illumination flows. There are numerous references in scripture to following Him as walking in the light. And we are even told that in heaven there will be no need for any light but Him. He is light embodied. And those who follow Him through earthly life will not have darkness but light.

JESUS, THANK YOU FOR BEING MY LIGHT. LET NO TINGE
OF DARKNESS CREEP INTO MY SPIRITUAL LIFE. AMEN.

GIFT

It is a good father's nature to give. Fatherlessness is greatly affecting our nation. The absence of biological dads and father figures in the community has crippled the manhood of many young men and done emotional damage in the hearts of young women. Fathers play a specific and vital role in their children's lives that mothers cannot fill. Fathers teach lessons moms can't. Fathers affirm their kids in ways mothers don't get. Fathers express love and instill confidence in their children in a manner that moms can't. And fathers give gifts to their children out of their desire to provide.

While there are many working mothers who help to take care of the needs of the family, it is usually the dads who feel the overwhelming need to make sure the family is clothed and sheltered. This seems to be the way God created the male psyche. And it is probably why Jesus referenced fathers and not mothers in this verse from Matthew. He knew that men were designed with this deep need to provide for those they love. And in using that analogy, He teaches us something wonderful about our heavenly Father.

He also wants to provide for us. And He will give us everything we truly need to live in relationship with Him. Human fathers are flawed and have imperfect understanding, and yet they give good things to their kids. How much more will the perfect, holy, heavenly Father give us good things if they help us to be the people He has willed us to be?

HEAVENLY FATHER, THANK YOU FOR PROVIDING FOR ME. I KNOW I
CAN TRUST YOU FOR WHAT I NEED TO GLORIFY YOU IN MY LIFE. AMEN.

It's funny, but I think of *Charlotte's Web* when I linger on the word *humble*. Remember the classic children's story? Templeton the rat is tasked with finding a word for the self-sacrificing spider to weave into her web in an attempt to save Wilbur's life. He returns from his nocturnal foraging with a scrap of paper bearing the word *humble*, and Charlotte dutifully spins her silk and writes the word. And the next morning, the world is astounded to see the message above the pigpen. The salvation of Wilbur the pig is in full swing.

I know a children's make-believe story isn't what God had in mind. However, the idea that humility attracts attention does carry over. God is drawn to our penitence and recognition of need. He does not come near the arrogant and proud but gives grace to the humble.

It is always better for Him to do the lifting up. He knows the best time and manner in which to do so. When we try to put ourselves in the position in which we believe we belong, we end up making a mess of the whole thing. It is much better for everyone involved, and certainly for His kingdom, for us to let Him decide whom to raise and whom to lower.

The Bible records the stories of those who did it both ways. King Nebuchadnezzar was reduced to a beast, roaming in the field and eating grass, because of his arrogance before the Lord. And David was exalted to be king because of his dependence on the Lord. God deals directly with the sin of pride. He stays His hand many times and calls us to repentance. But if we humble ourselves, we will still discover that He will lift us up according to His will.

LORD, ONLY YOU ARE FULLY WORTHY OF ESTEEM AND ADORATION.
HELP ME TO REMAIN HUMBLE IN YOUR SIGHT. AMEN.

VALUE

FEAR YE NOT THEREFORE, YE ARE OF
MORE VALUE THAN MANY SPARROWS.
Matthew 10:31

My grandmother kept parakeets. She loved those bright, domesticated birds and for a long time usually had one as a pet. I remember how she would clean the cage and change the food and water in it and cover it with a bath towel at night so the bird would go to sleep. And I remember that she liked to teach her parakeet friends to talk.

That's right. Like a parrot, a parakeet can learn to imitate sounds and produce understandable words. My grandmother found delight in teaching simple greetings and phrases to her birds. And as a child, I was fascinated. She valued her bird friends and did her best to take care of them. And when they died, she would bury them in a Velveeta cheese box and get another.

In telling His listeners about the value God places on human life, Jesus told those gathered that day that not even a single sparrow can lose its balance and plunge to its death on the ground below without God taking notice. (I guess that means God was aware every time one of my grandmother's parakeets died.) And then He follows that statement of omniscience with the words that human beings are worth more than many sparrows. If God is aware of the life cycle and daily activities of a bird, He is also aware of what is going on in our lives. And He places very high value on us. We are the ones He sent His Son to redeem. We are the ones on whom He wants to lavish His love. We are chosen and predestined for relationship with Him.

HEAVENLY FATHER, YOU KEEP TRACK OF ALL THE BIRDS AND YOU
KEEP TRACK OF ME. THANK YOU FOR LOVING ME THAT MUCH. AMEN.

O SING UNTO THE Lord A NEW SONG: SING UNTO THE Lord,
ALL THE EARTH. SING UNTO THE Lord, BLESS HIS NAME.
Psalm 96:1-2

Almost everyone imagines that they can sing. Many times, they are wrong.

In this age of unlimited music, when talent contests dominate the national fancy, many people consider themselves to have musical talent. But truly undiscovered virtuosos and prima donnas are scarce; however, it does happen. And that anomaly keeps tantalizing the Western mind with all the possibilities. We remember the moments when the ordinary housewife or the disabled teenager or the unassuming cabbie stepped up to the mic and glory poured forth. The tears in the eyes of the audience, the shock on the faces of the judges, the reward in the expressions of the family stay in our minds. We celebrate with them and think, *Why not me?*

Our God put special musical ability into many of His creation, but others are gifted in some other way. The wherewithal to produce magical vocal tones is simply not a universal talent. But regardless of ability, He wants us to sing to Him, using whatever voice we have, making a joyful melody unto Him for all He's done.

I once heard a Christian radio spot in which an off-key voice was heard, attempting to sing one of the great hymns on a Sunday morning. The voice-over proclaimed that when we hear that discord, God hears beautiful notes of praise; and in the background, the music became gorgeous swelling notes from a trained voice. I sometimes think of that when I hear songs of praise coming from someone who "can't carry a tune in a bucket." God wants to hear His people sing and bless His name with whatever voice they have.

LORD, HELP ME USE THE VOICE I HAVE TO PRAISE YOU IN SONG. AMEN.

KNOWN

GIVE THANKS UNTO THE Lord, CALL UPON HIS NAME,
MAKE KNOWN HIS DEEDS AMONG THE PEOPLE.
1 Chronicles 16:8

I'm a firstborn, and I take reassurance from what I know. They say that birth order plays into our personalities and our abilities and our moods. It affects how we approach life.

I recognized a few years back that knowledge means a lot to me. I feel confident if I have knowledge of the way something works or the reason behind what is happening in a relationship or situation. I even enjoy trivia because it broadens my understanding of a certain topic. Certainly not everyone is like that. If they were, we'd never make it through museums and historical sites because of the long queue to read the informational plaques!

However, God wants us to know some things. He wants us to know what He has done in the world for us and for those before us. Furthermore, He wants us to make sure others know it too. He is glorified when we call attention to His might and talk about the wonder of His works. This means that having conversations about intelligent design is important for more than refuting the heresy of evolution. Not only does it combat a lie, but it draws attention to what really happened—the God of the universe who deals in eternity crafted a world specially to nurture human life.

Of course, the greatest act that we can highlight is the plan of salvation, how God sent His only begotten Son, Jesus, to the world to be born, grow, live among us, teach us, die for us, and live again for us so that we can be reconciled in a personal relationship with Him. Not only does this message give the opportunity for others to receive Him, but it also brings glory to Him by making known what He has done for us.

FATHER GOD, I PRAISE YOU FOR YOUR GREAT DEEDS. I PLEDGE
ANEW TO MAKE THEM KNOWN TO OTHERS. AMEN.

Bullying is a scourge in any social setting. In recent years, there has been public attention drawn to this problem and a focus put forth to combat it. It is a sin no doubt as old as the first family, but that doesn't lessen its far-reaching effects.

Bullying is an evil act born in the heart of Satan for the destruction of humanity. The cruelty of bullying not only damages self-worth and inflicts unbelievable emotional pain, it also can result in injury and death when the victim lashes back in a violent way. All of this is what the enemy intends. He is overjoyed with any suffering he can instigate upon the human family.

The old adage of "sticks and stones can break my bones, but words can never hurt me" was probably created to help children combat the damaging influence of ugly words and names, but it should be more of a determination than a statement of fact. Words do hurt. And if the one at whom they are carelessly and cruelly hurled is already the recipient of little affirmation at home and no meaningful connection with God, that person will feel the pain even more deeply. This is not to say that Christians and those with good homes do not feel the hurt bullying brings, but rather that they have more resources with which to combat it and thus to numb the effect.

God, our Father, never bullies us. He is on the other side of that spectrum. He is on the giving side of grace and love and acceptance through Jesus Christ. He became the perfection we needed so that we can be accepted and reconciled to Him. In His Word, we find the love our souls need; and in relationship with Him, we discover unending peace.

FATHER GOD, THANK YOU FOR ACCEPTING ME THROUGH JESUS CHRIST. HELP ME TO BE A CHANNEL OF GRACE TO OTHERS. AMEN.

The word *victor* makes me think of the ancient games. Our modern fascination with sports probably is no more intense than in the days of the early church. The Romans had conquered the known world and had brought their love of conquest to the arenas of the day. In those huge, stadium-like buildings, chariots raced and gladiators fought to the death and yes, before long, Christians were martyred in the bloody sand. But for the games, victory was the prize, and a laurel wreath and the worship of those gathered were given to the champion.

A little, shrunken Dutch lady fought another type of battle hundreds of years after Rome fell. After being shipped to prison and then a cruel women's camp for helping rescue the Jews of Holland from Hitler's regime, Corrie ten Boom fought for daily survival in an atmosphere of horror, torture, and death. Along with her sister, Betsie, Corrie clung to the words of scripture against the very gates of hell, it seemed. And when Betsie succumbed to the ravages of disease and privation, and then Corrie herself was released, things were irrevocably changed. But she found the grace to keep going and began a speaking ministry in which she encouraged others to stand strong in their battles, inspiring them with her rally cry, "Jesus is Victor!"

And He is. He is Victor over sin, over temptation, over Satan, over death. There is nothing in which He cannot make us victorious also. He holds the keys of death and hell. He proclaims the message of victory to anyone who believes in His name. You can be victorious today through Him.

LORD JESUS, YOU HAVE WON THE ULTIMATE VICTORY. GIVE ME YOUR GRACE AND HELP SO THAT I CAN TRIUMPH TODAY. AMEN.

I DELIGHT TO DO THY WILL, O MY GOD:
YEA, THY LAW IS WITHIN MY HEART.
Psalm 40:8

Is there anyone more delighted with life in general than a two- or three-year-old? They find joy in simply existing, in waking up in their footed pajamas and running to wake up Mommy, in unrolling toilet paper in long streaming trails, in putting sticky handprints on the glass door. Yes, they can be willful and purposely destructive, but many of the things they get into are the result of natural curiosity and childish immaturity. They love to explore and delight in new sensory experiences.

I think God wants us to be like toddlers when it comes to following His will. People who reluctantly follow Christ make us feel that they believe a life of sin and self is actually better than living for the Savior.

The psalmist wrote that he found delight in doing the will of God, in following the precepts found in scripture. This is our model. How can we do this in practical ways?

- Develop an appetite for new truths in God's Word, like a toddler putting something in her mouth.

- Take notes in church so we can experience growth, like a preschooler who seemingly grows overnight.

- Wear an attitude of expectancy and joy, like a two-year-old pulls on a mismatching outfit and grins with the pure fun of her accomplishment.

- Look forward to the next step God shows us, like a little one explores new places with zest.

God teaches us many things through our observations of our world and the people in it. Today, resolve to find the delight of a toddler as you grow in Him.

FATHER, THANK YOU FOR HELPING ME GROW
THROUGH YOUR WORD AND THROUGH FELLOWSHIP
WITH OTHERS. I WANT TO DELIGHT IN YOU. AMEN.

THE Lord HATH DONE THAT WHICH HE HAD DEVISED; HE HATH
FULFILLED HIS WORD THAT HE HAD COMMANDED IN THE DAYS OF OLD.
Lamentations 2:17

Fulfilled has come to mean a kind of self-actualization. But in scriptural use, the word usually refers to God's accomplishment of His Word as He promised.

If there is one thing that encourages us in the Bible, it is the long list of stories where God came through for those He led. Over and over, His Word and His promises have been fulfilled:

- He brought Noah and his family through the flood.
- He gave Abraham a son.
- He brought the Hebrew nation out of slavery in Egypt.
- He conquered a giant with a sling in a shepherd's hand.

- He preserved His people through captivity and exile.

- He delivered Daniel from the lions and the three young men from a fiery furnace.

- He saved the Jewish nation from annihilation through a young queen.

- He proclaimed His power through the death of the martyrs.

- He shone His truth in the Reformation.

- He changed the known civilized world through the Great Awakening.

- He speaks today to those in oppressive regimes through visions and brings salvation where following Him is a crime.

Yes, God fulfills His Word. The verse for today says He does what He has devised. In other words, He created detailed plans to bring us back to Him and to glorify Himself on earth, and He is fulfilling it. Not one prophecy will be abandoned. Not one purpose of His will be left unfilled. We can trust Him.

FATHER GOD, I KNOW THAT YOU ACCOMPLISH ALL YOU SET OUT TO DO. PLEASE CONTINUE YOUR WORK IN ME. IN JESUS' NAME, AMEN.

HEART

The heart is the center of physical life. My husband suffered a heart attack at a young age. His was the type known as "the widowmaker." Many don't survive it. I am thankful God spared his life.

It happened unexpectedly when symptoms arose during a bike ride with our children. A few hours later found our family sitting bewildered in a hospital waiting room while medications were given and surgery was done and stents were inserted to alleviate the blockages. Then, when the immediate danger was past, we waited to hear the results of further testing. Was there significant and permanent damage to his heart?

Without the pumping of the physical heart, there is no life. We know, of course, that medical science has developed methods and machines to keep the heart beating. Defibrillation can shock the heart back into a rhythmic pattern even when it has stopped because of some type of trauma. Ventilators can keep the heart beating and the body fluids moving even when the brain is dead. Of course, it is possible for the body to be alive and there to be no ongoing life. In those instances, the family and medical team must decide to remove the artificial means of keeping the body going and let the spirit return to the God who gave it. But the fact remains that the heart is the machinery of life.

David, the psalmist, wrote that he would praise the Lord with his whole heart. We often use phrases like this in describing a deep commitment. To love someone else with your whole heart is the basis of marriage and family relationship. To adore our God through praise with every known purpose of our hearts is to give

Him the place He deserves in our lives. And like the physical heart keeps the body going, the devoted heart sends life to every fiber and muscle of our spiritual beings.

LORD, TODAY I WANT MY HEART TO BE IN RHYTHM WITH YOUR WILL. I LIFT UP MY PRAISE TO YOU WITH ALL MY BEING. AMEN.

MAKING REQUEST, IF BY ANY MEANS NOW AT LENGTH I MIGHT HAVE A
PROSPEROUS JOURNEY BY THE WILL OF GOD TO COME UNTO YOU.

Romans 1:10

Journaling is a trend today in the Christian community. Visit a Christian bookstore and you will find journals of many kinds. Some go along with popular studies and books on Christian living. Some simply provide scripture verses and daily entry pages to encourage personal reflection and growth through assimilation of the Word.

Journaling comes from the French root *jour*, meaning day. It is also the origin of the word *journey*. Both words have to do with something daily. To journey is to make steady progress, and to journal is to record a progression of events.

We often refer to our life in Christ as a Christian journey. Just as a traveler will come to difficult places along the way and then discover new vistas the next day, the follower of Christ will encounter various types of experiences as they make progress toward eternity.

The apostle Paul was a journeying man. He made many missionary journeys. In fact, many of our Bibles have a back page mapping out the journeys of Paul. He was accustomed to physical travel in his work for Christ. In the verse for today, He tells his readers in Rome that he was hoping to have a successful trip to visit them.

We know from later accounts and from history that Paul was later beheaded in Rome during the reign of Nero. And so one day the apostle took his final earthly journey, and then his soul winged its way into God's presence for eternity.

Today, your journey is leading you either closer to heaven or further from it. Like Paul's, may your final journey lead you beyond death and into His presence. And may the journals you leave behind bear testament to the God who led you all the way.

GOD ALMIGHTY, YOU HAVE PROVIDED A WAY FOR ME TO
JOURNEY IN FAITH THROUGH THIS LIFE AND ONE DAY BE
WITH YOU. I THANK YOU FOR THAT TODAY. AMEN.

GLORY

O Lord, our Lord, how excellent is thy name in all the earth! Who hast set thy glory above the heavens.

Psalm 8:1

Glory is a word reserved for shooting stars and brides on their wedding day and newborn cries. It's a word that captures an otherworldly type of awe and majesty.

When we talk about glory, it is often in a religious context. We don't often think of our human experiences as glorious. But those of us who know Christ have no trouble imagining that He has glory awaiting us. In fact, the old-timers used the word *glory* to describe heaven itself. Many old gospel songs speak of "going to glory."

American tradition also uses the word to describe the flag—the red, white, and blue. You will hear classic phrases like "Old Glory waving." This nickname came from the actual name given to the flag by a nineteenth-century sea captain named William Driver, who flew his red, white, and blue on his ships and later brought it to his home in Nashville, Tennessee. Today, two flags that are each purported to be Driver's originals are ensconced in the Smithsonian, preserved for posterity.

Why did Driver refer to his American flag as "Old Glory"? Probably because of the sense of awe it evoked in him and fellow patriots. There is something stunning about seeing our national colors waving proudly in the breeze. It stirs the blood and inspires the heart.

God intends for His creation to do the same in us. Today's verse comes from the eighth chapter of Psalms, where David is looking at the heavens in all their splendor. Surely the majesty of the created world draws attention to its Creator. Under the inspiration of the Holy Spirit, Paul declared in Romans 1 that, indeed, no one who can see the world around us is without proof of the existence of God. There is glory in every leaf and blossom and planet. His glory.

CREATOR GOD, I STAND IN AMAZEMENT AT THE MAJESTY OF YOUR
CREATION. YOUR GLORY IS ON DISPLAY ALL AROUND ME. AMEN.

MY SOUL FOLLOWETH HARD AFTER THEE:
THY RIGHT HAND UPHOLDETH ME.

Psalm 63:8

Surrender means giving in. It's difficult for us to do. It's always more gratifying to be the one whom others follow than it is to fall in behind someone else. At least it is for some temperaments. There are those who feel no need to make a statement, who don't want the work of being the leader, the trailblazer. But for many of us, there is just enough spirit and pride to make us desire to have the lead once in a while. And this quirky desire can show up in ordinary little ways like the delight we feel in sharing news no one at the table has yet heard. To be at the forefront of what is happening gives us a silly feeling of being important.

Without surrender to the information and authority of another, though, there would be little accomplished in our world. If every factory worker refused to submit to the working of the machinery and the route of the assembly line, chaos would take over and no product would emerge. If every medical student insisted on devising their own way to approach surgery, there would be much experimentation and death and little progress made through the adoption of others' methods. Having to do things "our" way can be a detriment to life, both in the physical world and in the spiritual one.

Surrender to God is a basic component of Christian living. In fact, we cannot even be in relationship with Him unless we acknowledge that we have sinned against His law (which is higher than our way) and then submit to His salvation and His will in us. Surrender is the crucible on which we succeed or fail in our Christian lives.

The writer of this verse just says it plainly: My soul follows intently after You. And when we adopt that approach, He will uphold us and lead us.

GOD, THANK YOU FOR SHOWING ME THAT YOUR WAY
IS PERFECT AND RIGHT. RIGHT NOW, I ACKNOWLEDGE
THAT I WANT YOU TO BE LORD IN ME. AMEN.

FOR THE LAMB WHICH IS IN THE MIDST OF THE THRONE SHALL FEED
THEM, AND SHALL LEAD THEM UNTO LIVING FOUNTAINS OF WATERS.
Revelation 7:17

Water fascinates us. It draws us to the ocean and natural places of beauty like Niagara Falls. Its power terrifies us in horrific hurricanes and floods. Its soothing effect beckons us to spend hours at the lake or by the pool. It affects us deeply.

The Bible often uses water to symbolize a spiritual concept. It is the fluid of life on earth. No kind of life can exist without it. Its absence on the moon accounts for some of the barrenness found there.

We know accounts from history where water made the difference between life and death. The settlers in the days of the Gold Rush and the westward expansion knew that one of the things they would encounter was a lack of water. They strapped large barrels to their covered wagons and schemed on how to make it from one town or well or lake to the next. When the supply got low, bathing ceased and water was rationed, the animals often getting their share before the people so that the caravans could continue on their journey. Skeletons of man and beast in our American deserts out West prove that they were not always successful in their quest.

In His conversation with a Samaritan woman by the side of a well one day, Jesus used water to symbolize the life He can put within us. He told her that He could give her living water so that she wouldn't thirst for the empty things she was then pursuing in her life. At first, she thought He was referring to the water from the primitive well where He sat. But instead, He was offering to satisfy her soul thirst with spiritual water that is never ending. And the verse today from Revelation continues that theme, promising that the Lamb, Jesus, will lead us into eternal joy, like an ocean of living water.

LORD, TODAY I HOLD UP MY THIRSTY SELF TO YOU.
SATISFY ME WITH YOUR LIVING WATERS. AMEN.

EVERY WORD OF GOD IS PURE: HE IS A SHIELD
UNTO THEM THAT PUT THEIR TRUST IN HIM.
Proverbs 30:5

When my brothers were young, they liked to make battle array. One of my brothers was especially adept at crafting homemade toys with which to engage in pretend battle. And of course, they needed a shield.

In ancient times, the shield was a vital piece of armor. In the heat of the battle, the shield could be raised to protect the bearer from attack, or it could be joined together with those around it to create an impenetrable wall of steel that allowed the men behind to advance in spite of the flying arrows.

Battles in ancient times were bloody affairs. Not that today's wars are not. But before the invention of weapons like guns, clashes between nations often came down to close combat fought with swords and knives. You were so close to your opponent that you could smell the fear and hate on him as distinctly as the raw blood that flowed on the ground around you. And you were glad for the shield in your hand that allowed you to deflect the blade he wielded.

This verse from Proverbs informs us that God is a shield to us and that every word of His is pure. He can protect us from the onslaught of doubt the enemy brings against us. And then we can discover the purity of His truth. Without that protection, we are at the mercy of Satan's lies. But with it, we are assured that we walk in truth—His truth.

LORD, THANK YOU FOR BEING MY SHIELD. I LOOK TO THE
PURE TRUTH YOU GIVE ME TODAY. IN JESUS' NAME, AMEN.

GOOD AND UPRIGHT IS THE Lord.

Psalm 25:8

"I'm good" is a common response. It doesn't refer to character but to condition.

Our grandparents wouldn't have understood our usage of this phrase today. In their day, the words *I'm good* meant "I am an upright person and I'm behaving properly." But in our generation, "I'm good" can mean I'm in a good mood, I have enough liquid in my glass, I'm satisfied with my life right now, and many other things.

But good is really a description of the nature of something. As a mom, you might admonish your children to "be good." You want them to follow a certain code of behavior. This is demonstrated in scripture by how the word is used to describe God. In its purest sense, *good* doesn't mean okay or mostly right; it means absolute and total uprightness. That's why Jesus challenged the young man we refer to as the "rich young ruler" when he approached Him with the title "Good Teacher." Jesus inquired why he singled Him out to be described as good. This indicated that the young man thought Jesus was holy and without any tinge of sin.

There is no one truly good except God. And while this word doesn't have the same connotation in our minds as it did in biblical times, we must recognize that what the writer says here is true. The Lord alone is totally good and fully upright. There is no flaw or blemish in His character, His intent, or His work.

....

....

....

....

HEAVENLY FATHER, BECAUSE YOU ARE GOOD, I CAN
TRUST YOU. I NEED NOT FEAR THAT YOU ARE HIDING EVIL
INTENTIONS. THERE IS COMPLETE HOLINESS IN YOU. AMEN.

BE STILL, AND KNOW THAT I AM GOD.

Psalm 46:10

The ability to sit still and be quiet is a skill that all of us must develop. It is in our nature to be distracted, especially now that we have our devices with us at all times, bringing the world to our fingertips at the swipe of a hand.

There have always been distractions, of course, to the human spirit. When the psalmist wrote these words, digital communication had not been discovered. There were no radios or screens or computers of any kind, but there were still disruptions to quiet because people are people and the world is a constant barrage of stimuli.

When my brother was young, he used to say that he was going to be a mountain man when he grew up. The idea of living in the wilderness appealed to him. I'm not sure that he wanted to be alone to be free of interaction with others, but that was often the intent of those men of yesteryear. Some of them were wanted by the law and just lost themselves in the forests and mountains. Some of them had reclusive and introverted dispositions and enjoyed solitude. Some of them just found themselves in that life after their families and communities were killed or died through disease. Whatever the cause, these men lived alone and died alone. I can't help but imagine that even they had to make it a point sometimes to quiet their own thoughts.

God tells us to discipline ourselves in the task of quietness. When our souls are still in His presence, we see His deity and power in new ways, and we are renewed.

HOLY GOD, I STILL MY MIND IN YOUR PRESENCE TODAY.
LET ME SEE YOUR POWER AND FEEL YOUR LOVE. AMEN.

SAVED

Don't you love to read stories about how someone's life was saved? It's always inspiring to read or hear the tale of how one person risked his life for another. There are countless ways in which this happens. It's common, of course, on the battlefield and in combat. Sometimes the hero survives and sometimes not. Often, they are awarded a posthumous medal for the bravery and selflessness shown in the act. At times, the account is from everyday life when something unexpectedly goes wrong in an ordinary day and a bystander reaches out a hand or plows through the debris of a car crash to save a human life. And then there are times when a large-scale tragedy occurs and emergency personnel and first responders and average citizens do everything they can to save others, such as happened in our country on September 11, 2001.

On that day in New York City, Washington D.C., and Shanksville, Pennsylvania, we witnessed the worst and best of human nature. Some men purposed to kill as many as they could. Others determined to save as many as possible. Firefighters braved fiery stairwells to lead others to life. Emergency personnel choked on the acrid fumes as they offered assistance to those fleeing the destruction. Passengers on a hijacked plane disdained their own chances and fought for the lives of others on the ground. We are still awed by the stories.

Yes, being saved from physical death is a wonderful thing, and often the one saved feels a deep bond to the one who went out of their way to make it possible. But being saved from spiritual death is of much greater importance, and the gratitude we have toward our Savior will be eternal. We can be saved from eternity in hell because of what He did for us.

....
....
....
....
....
....
....
....
....
....
....
....
....
....
....
....
....
....
....

LORD JESUS, YOU ARE MY SAVIOR FROM ETERNAL
DEATH, AND I WORSHIP YOU TODAY. AMEN.

FOR THEREIN IS THE RIGHTEOUSNESS OF GOD REVEALED FROM
FAITH TO FAITH: AS IT IS WRITTEN, THE JUST SHALL LIVE BY FAITH.
Romans 1:17

To be righteous is to be blameless, without fault. None of us can claim it on our own.

I love my automatic dishwasher. It saves me time, helps me keep my sink clear of dirty dishes, and makes the job of running my household a little easier. But sometimes, when I'm doing the not-so-fun task of emptying it, I come across a glass or a plate or a utensil that is not completely clean. It may have a film of grease on it or a little piece of food sticking to it, but it is not ready to be used again. It is not totally clean.

Usually, I'm the one at fault when that happens. I may not have scrubbed it well before putting it in the wash cycle, or maybe I totally overlooked its condition in my haste. Whatever. I brush it well and put it back in to go through again.

When God calls us to righteousness in Him, He intends for it to be total and complete. There is no room in His relationship with us for halfway purity. He doesn't want there to be any film or debris in our souls.

The world is okay with a little bit of dirt when it comes to the inner self. That's why you'll often hear the average person say, "Well, I'm a pretty good person." Or "I'm not really bad." There is usually a qualifying word involved. They recognize, by their own conscience, that they cannot claim complete goodness, but they are deceived into thinking that a little bit will be enough. God says no. Nothing but righteousness, total purity, will enter His kingdom. And He wants to work that in us by His grace.

LORD, YOUR WILL IS FOR ME TO BE RIGHTEOUS. COMPLETE THAT WORK IN ME SO I CAN STAND IN YOUR PRESENCE SOMEDAY. AMEN.

AND THOU SHALT BE SECURE, BECAUSE THERE IS HOPE.

Job 11:18

After being in the warmth of the womb for nine months, a newborn is unaccustomed to the free movement and cool air of the outside world. Medical science has discovered that newborns are comforted by tight wrappings around their bodies. They feel safe from falling and will be more content. No doubt the Native Americans discovered this long ago, and that is why we have discovered drawings of the boards and skins they used to bind the babies to the mothers' backs. Tightly bound to the one who gave them life, they swayed through the day and were lulled to contentment by the closeness. In the fields of agricultural countries, mothers created slings and other methods of holding their babies close and keeping their hands free. This allowed them to comfort the child and also do their work. Babywearing has experienced a revival today in America. Mothers have found out that they can get more done and have less stress if they keep the baby securely with them.

God's Word tells us that hope makes us feel secure. Just as a baby swaddled in warm cloths can relax in the mother's care, you and I, when we are wrapped in the hope that He gives, can rest, even in the midst of difficult circumstances.

If anyone understood the trials of life, it was Job, who lost everything he owned and almost his life during Satan's assault upon him. Yet he retained his trust and hope in God. And despite his miserable outward circumstances, he made it through, wrapped in the security of that reality.

FATHER GOD, WRAP ME TODAY IN THE COMFORT AND
SECURITY OF YOUR HOPE. I TRUST IN YOU. AMEN.

REPENT YE THEREFORE, AND BE CONVERTED, THAT YOUR
SINS MAY BE BLOTTED OUT, WHEN THE TIMES OF REFRESHING
SHALL COME FROM THE PRESENCE OF THE LORD.

Acts 3:19

Much of modern advertising is built on the "hook" of refreshment. Think about the ads you see every day on billboards and screens. Many of them offer some type of refreshing—in food, in drink, in leisure, in comfort.

Refreshment appeals to us. Our bodies are susceptible to weariness, hunger, thirst, and fatigue. We look for a way to satisfy those needs. It is often humorous, though, that the full-color ads are usually much better in picture than in reality. The burgers are always juicier in the commercials. The soft drink cans are always perfectly beaded with condensation and ice cold on the billboards. The vacations always seem more attractive in the flyers. Rarely does the actual experience equal or surpass what is promised. The allure of the tantalizing hope is usually greater.

God the Father promised times of refreshing to His people. These are not mere instances of having one's thirst slaked on a hot day. These are experiences of divine intervention in the human record. The verse from Acts tells us that these times would result in sins being forgiven. So we must look for them and pray for them and cooperate with His Spirit when they occur.

Throughout history, times of refreshing have come. God brought repentance and revival and refreshing when He allowed William Tyndale to translate the Bible into the common language of everyday people, when He let a German monk discover the truth that "the just shall live by faith," and when He used a couple of English brothers to avert a revolution in England.

He wants to bring times of refreshing today. And it will be more lasting than any modern convenience or comfort. His refreshing has eternal results.

LORD, LET YOUR REFRESHING WORK BEGIN IN ME TODAY. AMEN.

SURELY GOODNESS AND MERCY SHALL FOLLOW ME ALL THE DAYS OF MY LIFE: AND I WILL DWELL IN THE HOUSE OF THE Lord FOR EVER.

Psalm 23:6

"Mercy" used to be a common name for hospitals. Today we have corporate conglomerates that run our health care centers, but in the days past, many communities and towns had their own local hospitals. In one of the towns where I lived, there was a Mercy Hospital.

Mercy is a word that has more than one application. It can apply to the action of a judge in the sentencing of a convicted felon. It can describe the emotion of a nurse tending the wounded. It can be a plea for special consideration as when one sibling demands that the other yell "Mercy" when he's losing the fight. All of these situations involve a type of consideration for another, based not on what is deserved but on favor in the heart of the giver.

Most hospitals today have a code that instructs them to treat anyone, regardless of many restrictions—one of those being financial limitations. The mercy the hospital shows is demonstrated in their energetic attempts to save the life of any who walk through the doors. That mercy, however, is often retracted a bit when the bill arrives in the mail. Treatment may occur without interruption for ability to pay, but the day of reckoning comes sooner or later.

The mercy the Lord provides is free to us, but it cost Him the life of His Son. He was willing to send Him to the cross to suffer a criminal's death so that we could have abundant mercy. He knows we cannot pay, so He provided a way for the debt to be covered. And now, because of the redemption provided through Jesus, mercy is a constant companion as we walk with Him.

HEAVENLY FATHER, I DON'T DESERVE YOUR MERCY. YOU KNEW I COULD
NOT PAY THE DEBT, AND JESUS PAID IT FOR ME. THANK YOU. AMEN.

STAND FAST THEREFORE IN THE LIBERTY WHEREWITH CHRIST HATH MADE US FREE, AND BE NOT ENTANGLED AGAIN WITH THE YOKE OF BONDAGE.

Galatians 5:1

The human spirit longs for freedom. God built this principle into the very core of our existence.

We were created with the freedom of choice. God made humankind in His likeness with the ability to choose right from wrong. He did not need more angelic beings. He wanted beings who could choose relationship with Him.

Down through time, the story of humankind has been punctuated with the fight for freedom. Some of these struggles were built on a desire for domination by one nation and the desperate attempt to thwart it by another. As early as the Old Testament, we read about the countries who rose up to enslave and subjugate God's people. The time of captivity in Egypt was one such period. The people groaned under the oppression of their slave drivers and were forced to make bricks to build the empire of the Pharaoh. Other tyrants arose from Assyria and Persia and Philistia and Rome, intent on conquering the nation of Israel. And often they succeeded.

In the history of the world at large, the struggle for freedom continued. Alexander the Great conquered the known world and cried because he had no further conquest. Napoleon Bonaparte set out to make a name for himself in the list of great leaders. Stalin, Hitler, and Lenin all had a lust for more land and more power. And surely no struggle for freedom is more acclaimed than America's own War for Independence, backed up by a declaration that these "colonies ought to be free and independent states."

Yes, the struggle for freedom is inherent in the human story. But there is a greater freedom we are offered through the blood of Christ. He has died to give us freedom from our enemy, Satan. Because of Christ's redemptive work, we have liberty both in this life and in the one to come. Not liberty to indulge selfish tendencies, but liberty to live for Him.

LORD, THANK YOU FOR THE LIBERTY PROVIDED
THROUGH CALVARY. I STAND IN IT TODAY. AMEN.

We are called sheep in scripture. And sheep need someone to follow. It's not a very glamorous analogy. Sheep have little motivation of their own and not much sense. They don't have the intelligence to keep from getting lost or getting into danger.

Shepherding was a common profession in biblical times. Wealthy families often had their own shepherd. Those who had little would use the community shepherd, who would take the flocks out for grazing days at a time.

We enjoy reading the stories of famous shepherds in the scriptures. Moses tended sheep on Mount Sinai and encountered God through a burning bush. David cared for his father's sheep and perfected his skills with his slingshot, which God used to bring down the heathen Goliath. In these instances, God taught His men important lessons as they took care of these mild but unflattering animals.

Jesus looked out on the people of His day with compassion and thought of them as sheep without a shepherd. They were wandering far from God, not realizing how to truly know Him. They followed earthly rabble-rousers who encouraged them to seek an earthly kingdom instead of a heavenly one. And in His death and by His love, He became the Great Shepherd.

Today, as in His day, the people of our world are scattered, following one voice after another. We can help to bring them to the Shepherd who can show them the path of life. We who know His voice follow Him into life and righteousness and honor. And there is always room to bring others with us.

....

....

....

....

....

....

....

....

....

....

....

....

....

....

LORD, YOU ARE THE GREAT SHEPHERD, AND TODAY I
RENEW MY COMMITMENT TO FOLLOW YOU. AMEN.

CONFESS YOUR FAULTS ONE TO ANOTHER, AND PRAY
ONE FOR ANOTHER, THAT YE MAY BE HEALED.

James 5:16

Confession is not usually pleasant. But the results are healing. Most mothers have had the experience of hearing a crash and going to investigate the damage. There, among the shards, may be more than one wide-eyed face. The question is asked: "Who did it?" It's confession time.

Confession is difficult for us because it requires us to own up to guilt. And none of us like to admit that we are flawed. That's wrongful pride, and it's the main reason why many refuse to come to God for salvation. They are not willing to admit that they need a Savior. They cannot squelch their pride enough to reach out for help.

Confession is an admission not only of guilt but, at times, of need. When people struggling with an addiction come clean to a support group, they are saying, "I can't handle this on my own. I need help." This also strikes at the pride within us. We innately want to solve our own problems and make our own way. This is the twisting of self-centeredness caused by sin in our world.

To be in relationship with God requires that we confess first to Him. We must acknowledge our inability to save ourselves from sin and reach out for the work Jesus did on Calvary for us. The Bible admonishes us to confess our shortcomings and struggles to other believers and find support in their love and prayers. It is humbling to make a confession, and I think that's what God intends anyway. The idea that we can make it on our own originated with Satan, and it leads straight to eternity alone in hell. But confession leads to healing and life and peace with Him and others. It's the way to go.

LORD, I CONFESS MY NEED OF YOU TODAY. DEVELOP IN ME THE HUMILITY I NEED TO DEPEND ON YOU. IN JESUS' NAME, AMEN.

AS SNOW IN SUMMER, AND AS RAIN IN HARVEST,
SO HONOUR IS NOT SEEMLY FOR A FOOL.

Proverbs 26:1

Harvest is a time of celebration. The crops are in and the worry is past. There is plenty. There is feasting. There is joy.

Harvest is a biblical theme, but we owe much of our understanding of the joy of the harvest to an American tradition called Thanksgiving. Schoolchildren learn of the indomitable pilgrims who battled through the "starving time" and the diseases of their little community. They were finally providentially rescued by Native Americans who taught them the fine points of growing crops in the New World. When the danger had passed and a bountiful harvest was gained, the people rejoiced and celebrated with a feast that lasted for days and that provided enough for everyone. In this story, we find a real-life example of the joy of plenty. Harvest has always been a respite from want and worry.

In ancient times, harvest was also celebrated. Heathen cultures often intertwined occultic and perverted rituals into their times of feasting. They did not recognize the fact that the Lord God gives food to all the earth. But for the people of God, harvest has provided a natural season in which to give thanks to whom it belongs—our heavenly Father.

The Proverbs writer asserts that snow is not proper in summer nor rain in harvest. The days of the harvesting should be warm and dry to allow for proper storage of the crops. The conditions of the weather greatly affect the product of the harvest, not only on the farm but in our souls.

God wants to cultivate His harvest in us, a harvest of godliness and peace and love for others. And He celebrates when He sees the bounty of His grace in us.

HEAVENLY FATHER, I THANK YOU FOR THE HARVEST OF THE
NATURAL WORLD AND FOR THE HARVEST YOU PLAN IN ME. AMEN.

FOR AS HE THINKETH IN HIS HEART, SO IS HE.
Proverbs 23:7

To reflect is to mirror back. Before the days of modern mirrors, humans peered into water and shiny surfaces to catch their image. These were shadowy representations at best. And early mirrors were sometimes wavy and distorted, not giving a clear picture of the person looking into them. Today, you can buy a good mirror for a dollar. We are inundated with reflections of ourselves.

Babies are intrigued with their own images. The other day I was talking to a young parent who said that his child was fascinated with her own reflection. Is it an innate recognition of the Creator's image that enthralls them? We know their developing sense of self-awareness is triggered by seeing the human face. But why are they more thrilled with their own image than with that of another?

I'm told that people in primitive lands are likewise spellbound at the sight of their own reflection in a mirror. Of course, many of them have never seen themselves at all! Imagine what it would be like to see yourself for the very first time.

Most of us have many mirrors in our possession. It is a common thing to check our appearance, and we do it regularly. It's considered a proper part of good hygiene and self-care. But have you considered that you should be checking out your internal reflection on a regular basis as well?

The Word of God is a mirror that reflects what we look like on the inside. It is never distorted and shadowy. It always tells the unvarnished, untouched truth. Our verse for today reminds us that, as we think in our hearts, so is our true nature. Let's check that reflection today.

GOD, SHOW ME MY TRUE NATURE TODAY THROUGH YOUR
WORD. I WANT MY REFLECTION TO HONOR YOU. AMEN.

BLESSED ARE THEY WHOSE INIQUITIES ARE
FORGIVEN, AND WHOSE SINS ARE COVERED.
Romans 4:7

When my children were little and were unkind to each other, they were required to grant forgiveness when asked.

A long time ago, I heard a preacher or teacher explain that to receive an apology with "That's okay" was actually an avoidance of giving forgiveness. If one can just pass off the offense without offering pardon, it may not be truly forgiven. It is good for us to say the words "I forgive you," because it forces the issue on us.

I don't think my children actually enjoyed this exercise in discipline, but I hope it taught them a valuable lesson. Forgiveness is something we offer by choice and not by feeling. We don't have to be overwhelmed with warm fuzzies to forgive someone. In fact, feelings are just not part of the equation. Forgiveness means "I let you off the hook."

God didn't just overlook our sins when He adopted us into His family. He provided the payment for our debt by sending Jesus to be our substitute sacrifice. Because of this, He offers us full and complete forgiveness. He'll never say "Oh, it's nothing" when we confess, because it *is* something. Sin is always terrible and demands a high price. But He can cancel the debt because of the cross, and His Word promises that He forgives anything we confess to Him by faith.

OH GOD, THANK YOU FOR TAKING CARE OF MY
DEBT AND FOR FORGIVING ME FOR JESUS' SAKE. AMEN.

HONOR

HONOUR THY FATHER AND MOTHER; WHICH IS THE
FIRST COMMANDMENT WITH PROMISE.
Ephesians 6:2

Often, there will be an honor guard at military funerals. Those of us who like ceremony and pageantry relish this display of beauty even during a time of grief. There is comforting splendor in the impeccably dressed officers, the gleaming steel of the weapons, the stiff-armed slant of the salutes, the shrill tones of "Taps," and the tight wrap of the American flag. All of these things are done in honor of the deceased. A sloppy presentation does not do justice to the service of the person being remembered. Only sharp and orderly angles and manners and actions will suffice.

For recruits going into basic training (or boot camp as it used to be known), learning how to be expertly shined and polished and prepared is an important part of their new job. I've heard stories of quarters flipped onto bunks to check the tightness of the wrap and white gloves used for inspection of weaponry. And every raw recruit quickly learns the value of highly polished boots and a pressed uniform during inspection. These things bring honor to the ranks and to the officers and to the country.

The word *honor* is used many times in scripture. In the verse for today, it refers to the actions and attitudes one should display toward parents. When we are young, our fathers and mothers put us through "boot camp." At least, some form of it. They teach us that respect is expected and proper, and they show us how they want us to take care of ourselves and our surroundings and respond to them. When we are older and on our own, we still need to be able to pass inspection at a moment's notice. There is no season of life when our honor guard can retire.

....

....

....

....

....

....

....

....

....

....

....

....

....

....

....

....

....

....

....

HEAVENLY FATHER, I WANT TO PROPERLY HONOR THOSE
YOU HAVE GIVEN ME AS PARENTS. THANK YOU FOR
TEACHING ME THROUGH YOUR WORD. AMEN.

OBEY MY VOICE, AND I WILL BE YOUR GOD,
AND YE SHALL BE MY PEOPLE.

Jeremiah 7:23

When we had an unruly and energetic Golden Lab pup, we longed to send her to obedience school. Friends recommended it highly. They gushed about the difference it would make. We were tantalized by the thought of the lovable, mild-mannered family pet she could become, but we never did it.

Dogs, like people, have their own ideas about how to do things. The problem with our Molly was that we didn't come on strong in the beginning. To be fair, we got her when she was already several weeks old, so we didn't have the luxury of training her from birth. Still, having never before encountered a pet like her, we were unprepared to deal with her hyperactive disposition as well as her stubborn desire to do things her way. It is funny that she was not unlike a human toddler in many aspects of her behavior. The answer, of course, was discipline, and she could have been taught, but it would take time and patience.

We also must learn obedience. As children, our parents want to help us understand that doing what they say will give us the best life possible. They are there to train us, educate us, and prepare us. Learning obedience also sets us up to submit to God's authority in our spiritual lives. There must be instant focus when He speaks and a commitment to doing what He says.

In humans, part of the battle is in helping children be motivated to obey. We want them to *want* to obey. This starts with persuasion through discipline, but we hope it is finalized in their hearts by a growing yearning to please the parent by obedience. And this is what God wants in His children as well.

HEAVENLY FATHER, YOU ARE TEACHING ME TO LISTEN
TO YOUR VOICE AND OBEY YOUR COMMANDS. THANK
YOU FOR YOUR PATIENCE WITH ME. AMEN.

FOCUS

As a teacher, I have found one of the most irritating traits in my students to be a lack of focus. You know what I mean. The student who gazes out the window instead of looking at his textbook or the one who idly flips her pencil while staring blankly at the board up front. The lack of focus is obvious and detrimental to learning.

A tried-and-true trick in every teacher's arsenal is the "call the student's name out loud" strategy. Suddenly addressing a specific question to the star-gazing student can snap him or her back to reality and sometimes help with focus. And there are other means with which to pull the student back into the classroom. Physical presence or moving closer to stand beside the student's desk sometimes works. Putting together study groups and allowing for interaction can help those who need verbal input to focus. Varying the lesson presentation with lecture, media, and student participa-tion is also a good idea.

But in the end, students must learn the discipline of focus for themselves. There is no one who can force another person to center their mind on the subject at hand.

Jesus was focused on our redemption. Through all He endured, He had His gaze squarely fixed on the cross and the work He had to do there. Everything else was part of the path that led there. The writer of Hebrews tells us that He endured torture and humiliation, and He suffered the shame of a public and excruciating death. He would not let anything deter Him from finishing the Father's plan.

You and I must be focused as we live for Him every day. The Holy Spirit, our faithful teacher, will do all He can to help us learn. But it is our responsibility to fix our eyes on Him and then complete the path He has laid out for us.

LORD GOD, THANK YOU FOR GIVING ME THE EXAMPLE OF JESUS TO FOLLOW. TODAY I FOCUS MY GAZE ON HIM. AMEN.

179

Angels

BE NOT FORGETFUL TO ENTERTAIN STRANGERS: FOR
THEREBY SOME HAVE ENTERTAINED ANGELS UNAWARES.

Hebrews 13:2

We are intrigued by angels. Books, figurines, television shows, and personal accounts abound on the existence and work of angels.

When I was a child, a picture hung on the wall of my bedroom. It showed a boy and girl crossing a bridge at night. There was a raging torrent below, and there were boards missing on the bridge. The stars were shining overhead, and the children were huddled together as they seemed to inch their way to the other side. But towering behind them, with flowing golden tresses, beautiful robes, white feathery wings, and a jewel on her forehead was a lovely angel, guiding them to safety.

I loved this picture and still do. Not because of its accuracy. Angels probably don't really look like that. And what in the world were those children doing out at night anyway? But no matter, the point is that angels are God's messengers, and they often assist us in unseen ways.

The Bible mentions angels that we refer to as guardian angels. It talks of the announcing angel, Gabriel, and the warrior angel, Michael. The heavenly "host" is often referenced in scripture. Yes, angels are real and have an important role in God's realm.

Today's verse presents an intriguing thought. We are told that angels might appear in the form of a stranger and show up at our homes. That's quite a good reason to take your hospitality seriously. In fact, the New Testament advises Christians to offer hospitality. God is in the business of welcome, and He wants us to be as well.

I don't know if you will have any angelic encounters this week or if you will recognize them if you do, but be assured that God's messengers are on your side, and they do the bidding of the One who loves you most and best.

GOD IN HEAVEN, I'M GLAD FOR YOUR ARMY OF HEAVENLY
BEINGS WHO WORK FOR YOU. THANK YOU FOR SENDING
THEM TO HELP ME WHEN I NEED IT. AMEN.

THAT IF THOU SHALT CONFESS WITH THY MOUTH THE LORD
JESUS, AND SHALT BELIEVE IN THINE HEART THAT GOD HATH
RAISED HIM FROM THE DEAD, THOU SHALT BE SAVED.
Romans 10:9

Belief is the action of grace. Many times we hear someone say "I don't believe it!" or "Can you believe it?" What they are actually expressing is incredulity at what they have just heard. Their minds are not willing to embrace the facts or story they've just been told.

The early explorers and inventors faced this same kind of resistance. In long-ago times, it was commonly thought that the earth was flat. Scholars of the day were convinced that it was not possible to sail around the earth because the ship would fall off the edge. Ferdinand Magellan proved this wrong when he sailed around the world, but for years those who suggested such an idea were scoffed at.

It was also believed that maggots came from meat, but Francesco Redi showed that flies laid the eggs from which the worms came. And in the early days of medicine, there was no concept of germs and bacteria. Doctors treated patients with unwashed hands, and conditions were not kept sanitary; many died of secondary infection. All of these ideas were new and wild theories at one time, but they were proven to be true. And practices and methods changed to accommodate the beliefs.

We are told to believe with our hearts in Jesus as our Savior. This is more than mere mental assent. It is a kind of belief that causes us to change our practices and embrace a new way of doing things. Belief is not works, but it is action. It is an energetic, decisive choice to follow Christ, and it results in eternal life.

LORD, I HAVE BELIEVED IN YOU FOR CLEANSING AND FOR ETERNAL LIFE. LET MY ACTIONS TODAY PROVE THAT MY BELIEF IS REAL. AMEN.

BLESSED IS THE NATION WHOSE GOD IS THE Lord; AND THE
PEOPLE WHOM HE HATH CHOSEN FOR HIS OWN INHERITANCE.

Psalm 33:12

"Choose teams." These words uttered on the playground can produce dread in the heart of a child. It did in me. I did not want to stand on the auction block of recess, being evaluated for my athletic prowess. I knew I would come up short in that review, and I was usually right. You know how it is. When you get to the end, the team captains say, "Okay, I'll take _____ and you get _____." It's like saying "Let's divide the dead weight between us."

All of us want to be chosen. We want to be valued, appreciated for what we can bring to the team. But many of us didn't have that affirmation in our school days. In fact, many of us haven't had that affirmation in our adult lives. We've never been chosen first for anything. We've always been relegated to last pick, left for the vultures of life to scrape off the pavement after the best has been devoured.

But Jesus has chosen us. First. For His own. He wants relationship with each one of us. After all, there is no duplicate of you. You're the only one. So if He says He's chosen you, that really means you, not the rest of the population, but you as an individual. He has chosen you to experience His love and grace and eternal life. He has chosen you as a recipient of His inheritance. In Christ, you are a chosen person.

LORD, THANK YOU FOR CHOOSING ME TO KNOW YOU. AMEN.

PLEASANT WORDS ARE AS AN HONEYCOMB, SWEET
TO THE SOUL, AND HEALTH TO THE BONES.
Proverbs 16:24

One of the tastes we can distinguish with our tongues is sweetness. It's funny that most of the things we think we taste are actually smells. Science tells us that the human tongue can distinguish four things—sweetness, saltiness, bitterness, and sourness. All the rest of our delight in food comes through our olfactory glands—our sense of smell.

That means the incredible Italian meal doesn't really taste good but rather smells good. The chocolate chip cookies, warm from the oven, are mostly a smelling experience. The fresh rolls at Sunday dinner are a combination of smell and texture. It kind of messes with your vocabulary and your basic thoughts about eating.

Honey and honeycomb in the Bible are usually associated with sensory delight. It was a treat in ancient days to have honey. That's why Samson was willing to risk his Nazarite vows to retrieve the honey from the lion's carcass. It was a rare treat. The psalms even compare God's Word to honey and honeycomb, pleasant to the taste and a treat for the senses.

The writer of Proverbs was inspired to write that pleasant words are like a honeycomb and healthy for the bones. This tells us that God can use our kind and affirming words. When we choose our words well, we become a source of sensory delight that He can use to sweeten the day of someone else. That's pretty awesome.

....
....
....
....
....
....
....
....
....
....
....
....
....
....
....
....
....
....
....
....
....
....
....
....
....

FATHER GOD, HELP ME BE AWARE OF MY WORDS TODAY.
USE THEM TO SWEETEN ANOTHER'S LIFE. AMEN.

THE RIGHTEOUS SHALL FLOURISH LIKE THE PALM TREE:
HE SHALL GROW LIKE A CEDAR IN LEBANON.

Psalm 92:12

Palm trees grow up. Many kinds of trees spread out as they grow. Palm trees usually are tall and spindly with frothy fronds sprouting from the top. One of the delights of visiting a tropical or subtropical climate is the change in the foliage and flora and fauna. I have enjoyed trips to Florida, where the smell of the salt air is a tangy reality and the gritty sand reminds me I'm not in Kansas anymore! And I always relish my first glimpse of a palm tree. So different from the chunky coniferous and deciduous trees farther north, these stately plants seem to hold court over the sunny empire of the sea.

In the Middle East, where most of the happenings of the Bible occurred, there were palm trees, and the psalmist used them as a visual for the growth of the righteous. No doubt they were scattered over the landscape and around the desert oases and grew very tall, their roots having to dig down deep to find a water source. There were also the famous cedar trees of Lebanon, used in building Solomon's temple for the Lord. There were no others like them. They were special.

Christians are constantly growing. There is never a time when they stop sinking their roots deeper or quit reaching toward the sun of God's grace. They flourish like the palm trees and grow strong like the cedar trees. And they stand as testaments to His power at work in them.

LORD, I WANT TO FLOURISH FOR YOU. PLANT ME
WHERE YOU WILL AND HELP ME GROW. AMEN.

The Bible portrays richness in both positive and negative light. Many of the saints of the Old Testament were rich men—Abraham, Isaac, Jacob, Job, David, etc. They were not looked down on because of it. It was merely part of who they were. And God used it.

In the New Testament, Jesus often warned against riches and certainly against trusting in them. He even said it was difficult for a rich man to enter the kingdom of God. And the young ruler who came to Jesus turned away because the Bible tells us he had many riches.

Still, the Bible itself does not condemn wealth if it is used in the proper way. We are told not to trust in material wealth because it is uncertain. Yet we are admonished to be good stewards, to use what we have been given, and even to store up in a wise way in case bad days come.

Certainly, the riches that the Bible commends are spiritual and eternal. Parables like the one Jesus told about the pearl of great price encourage us to keep a proper focus on what really matters. In the Sermon on the Mount, Jesus said we need not be unduly worried about what we will eat and wear because the Father in heaven will take care of us. He warned against trying to serve both God and material gain. One or the other will take precedence.

Most of us do not have to worry that we will be vastly wealthy. But we do have to stay on our guard against the desire always to have more and to be discontent. We need to place our focus on the true riches found in the wisdom and knowledge of God.

FATHER GOD, THANK YOU FOR THE RICHES OF YOUR GRACE. HELP ME FOCUS ON WHAT REALLY MATTERS. AMEN.

WHEN HE, THE SPIRIT OF TRUTH, IS COME, HE
WILL GUIDE YOU INTO ALL TRUTH.
John 16:13

In the early days of American history, a guide was necessary for those taking trips into new territory. Remember Lewis and Clark? We learned about them in elementary school and about their fascinating Native American guide, Sacagawea. With her baby strapped to her back, she helped the white men find their way to the Pacific. But things didn't always turn out so well. The wrong guide was the reason for the disaster of the Donner party in the Sierra Nevadas of California.

Today, we also have a guide with us all the time. It's called a GPS, a global positioning system. Little mechanisms in our phones that are connected with infrastructure around the world help us navigate in ways our ancestors couldn't have imagined.

Even with my GPS, I can get turned around. Maybe it's just me, since I am directionally challenged, but there are times where the screen is hard to read, when the track it's showing me seems to go in a lane of traffic different from what the woman's voice is saying. So I've had to find a place to turn around even while using my GPS.

The Holy Spirit is the Spirit of truth. Everything He says is true. Everywhere He leads is right. There is no need to doubt or consult another system or turn around. Jesus even said that it was better for the Holy Spirit to be with us than to have His physical presence. The Spirit of God can be everywhere at once and can actually live inside us; we are never without His guidance if we are in relationship with the Father. There is no better guarantee against getting lost than that!

HOLY SPIRIT, GUIDE ME INTO TRUTH AND SHOW
ME THE RIGHT PATHS TO TAKE. AMEN.

AND THE GRACE OF OUR LORD WAS EXCEEDING ABUNDANT
WITH FAITH AND LOVE WHICH IS IN CHRIST JESUS.
1 Timothy 1:14

Do you like surprises? Some of us do and some of us don't. I like certain surprises, but if I am unprepared for the situation that unfolds because of the surprise, I'm not a big fan of it.

My husband is very hard to fool with a surprise. I've succeeded a few times but not as much as I'd like. I tell him it's because he has a suspicious mind (smile). But he is also of the opinion that surprises aren't as much fun as anticipation. When planning a party for someone else to celebrate a significant event, why not tell them in advance so they can look forward to it? That makes sense.

Of course, there are some occasions when a surprise works out perfectly and would have been spoiled by prior knowledge. In those instances, the unexpected joy is a real delight.

The grace of our Lord is a surprise to many of us. Oh, we know that He has promised it, and we have heard from others that it is wonderful, but when we experience it for ourselves, we are amazed. Perhaps you've heard the testimony of those who have gone through great trials or experienced terrible tragedy. They usually say something about the grace "being there when you need it." You believe them of course. But it's only when you experience it that you are astounded by the abundance of it. Those who are martyred for their faith surely experience something like that. While none of us can know while we're living, and they can't come back to tell us, it must be that the overwhelming grace and strength of God comes to them in those horrible, final moments in a way we cannot imagine when we don't need it. Stephen, the first Christian martyr, saw Jesus standing to receive Him. That sure sounds like grace to me!

OH GOD, THANK YOU THAT THE GRACE I NEED WILL BE
THERE IN ABUNDANCE AT THE RIGHT TIME. AMEN.

GREAT IS THY FAITHFULNESS.
Lamentations 3:23

I like things that don't fail. I want my central air to stay on, my washing machine to chug away, my dishwasher to stay functional, my water heater to continue blazing, and my electricity to shoot through the wires.

When my son took a mission trip, he was told that the power on the mission compound was erratic. This is common in other countries that have more primitive conditions and less dependable infrastructure. We are often unprepared for the realities of living in an environment where things don't work well. Americans are prone to expect things to be efficient and workable at all times. And that's because it is normally how things go in our country.

People of former times were much better at adapting to unexpected outages and shortages. In fact, those who lived through the Great Depression excelled at doing much with little. They learned to be flexible and inventive and kept going despite the hardships.

In the spiritual realm, we need never be afraid that God won't be faithful. His very nature is faithfulness, and He will always be true to His character. There hasn't been nor will there ever be a moment when He isn't who He claims to be or when He backs out on a promise or when He changes His mind about His covenant.

All through the Bible, we are given examples of His faithfulness. We are reminded that He is faithful in every generation and to every person in it. No one will be able to claim that they were the exception. God's faithfulness doesn't fail. Ever.

HEAVENLY FATHER, YOU ARE CONTINUALLY AND ALWAYS FAITHFUL. I PRAISE YOU FOR THAT TODAY. AMEN.

AS FOR GOD, HIS WAY IS PERFECT: THE WORD OF THE LORD IS
TRIED: HE IS A BUCKLER TO ALL THOSE THAT TRUST IN HIM.
Psalm 18:30

A perfect 10. A 4.0. A 100 percent. An A+. These are the measurements of excellence. Humans have devised numerical scales for determining perfection. How they came into being is another discussion. The fact is, we all know the criteria for making the top tier.

I was an overachiever in school and unhappy with anything less than an A. As a parent, I tend to expect my children to excel if they are able, and I urge them toward the top. I have tried not to make it an unattainable goal. However, I believe that high expectation usually precedes high achievement.

My children have been blessed with academic ability and mental clarity and have not experienced great difficulty in maintaining good grades. But when my oldest daughter entered nursing school, she discovered that she had to adjust her own expectations. There is no cause for giving up, but there are some areas of learning where the most important thing may not be making an A but just making it through! As she has accepted the fact that the medical field is academically challenging, she has been able to celebrate her best even if it would have been unacceptable to her in former years.

Wherever we find ourselves on the scale of human achievement, there is one thing of which we can be certain. The Lord's way is perfect, and His Word needs no improvement. Time cannot make it better. We can trust in the excellence of everything He does.

FATHER, I'M SO GLAD FOR THE PERFECTION OF YOUR
WORD AND YOUR WAY. I TRUST YOU. AMEN.

DREAM

A dream doesn't have to happen at night. Most of us know about daydreams. Sometimes they are an escape from reality. Other times, they are a growing awareness of a path we want to take.

Little in this life happens without someone first having a dream about it—not a dream while they're sleeping but a dream to make something a reality. Great inventions begin this way. Modern improvements are born this way. Philosophical change comes about this way. Humanitarian progress occurs this way. A dream about change and progress can result in great accomplishment and victory.

Of course, dreams can also bring about negative events. Most of the despots and tyrants of history have daydreamed about control and power and domination. So dreams aren't necessarily a good thing. They are only good if the one doing the dreaming has good intentions.

God tells us in His Word that He has dreams about us. Well, we can say it that way in human language. He has plans for us, and they are plans of peace and a good ending. This promise was originally given to the nation of Israel, but because salvation is now opened to all, we are included in its beautiful hope.

Today, let the assurance that God dreams about your future bring you comfort and joy.

....

....

....

FATHER GOD, THANK YOU FOR GIVING ME REASON TO
LOOK FORWARD TO A FUTURE WITH YOU. AMEN.

Presence

AND YE SHALL SEEK ME, AND FIND ME, WHEN YE
SHALL SEARCH FOR ME WITH ALL YOUR HEART.
Jeremiah 29:13

Hide-and-seek. It's a game babies love. It's delightful to watch infants catch on to the rhythm of hide-and-seek. The fun in their baby eyes is awesome, and the way they chortle with glee when they see a face suddenly peeking at them from behind a blanket is such a happy sound. Perhaps you have played this little game with your own children or with a niece or nephew, grandchild, or other little friend. The joy the child feels is surely not as great as the delight the adult enjoys in seeing the pleasure on the younger one's face and in seeing the baby catch on to how it works.

I think this must be the way God feels about us when we seek Him. Except He has promised that He won't hide Himself from our search. In fact, He promises to be easy to find.

Remember when you played this game with elementary friends? It wasn't a baby game anymore. It was a challenge to see who could remain hidden the longest, and oh, the lengths to which we could go!

But God isn't like that. He wants us to discover Him and get to know Him. He went to all the sacrifice of sending His only beloved Son to show us what He was like, and now He will continue to help us along as we search for Him.

If we seek Him with all our hearts, He has promised to let us find Him. Are you searching today?

FATHER IN HEAVEN, I WANT TO GET CLOSER TO YOU
TODAY. THANK YOU FOR HELPING ME DO THAT. AMEN.

A WISE MAN WILL HEAR, AND WILL INCREASE LEARNING; AND A MAN OF UNDERSTANDING SHALL ATTAIN UNTO WISE COUNSELS.

Proverbs 15

"Put on your listening ears!" This is an admonishment we give to young students. It helps them remember to close their mouths and use their ears. Someone has wisely said that we have two ears and only one mouth, which should tell us that we need to listen twice as much as we talk. If adults could remember this, we would also be better off.

There are many reminders in scripture to listen. We are told to listen to our mothers and fathers, to wise counsel, to the elderly, to prophets and preachers, to the call of wisdom, to the words of the law, to the voice of the Great Shepherd, and to the instruction of the Holy Spirit. Jesus often made comments about having "ears to hear." It seems He was saying that we should purposefully listen to the things in the Word.

Mothers sometimes refer to "selective hearing." This means that children seem to tune out parents' voices and words at certain times, hearing only what they want to hear. We as God's children must not be guilty of that. There are certain times when the truth is hard to hear, yet we must not search for someone who tells us what we want to hear but instead embrace the truth and make whatever adjustments are necessary. The writer of Proverbs says that the wise person will hear on purpose and will increase in learning. Let's make that the goal today.

LORD, I PROPOSE TODAY TO HEAR ON PURPOSE THE TRUTH
YOU BRING TO ME. THANK YOU FOR YOUR WORD. AMEN.

THE LORD HATH HEARD MY SUPPLICATION;
THE LORD WILL RECEIVE MY PRAYER.
Psalm 6:9

"I don't want charity." There are those who have a difficult time receiving from another. It may spring from a fierce desire to be independent. It may arise from years of having to accept castoffs from others and being humiliated that they were the community "do-good" project. Accepting a gift or help is almost more than they can bear.

Most of us don't have any trouble receiving gifts on our birthdays or at Christmas. In fact, we expect to receive free stuff at these times! Yet in some countries, the one having the birthday gives gifts. And often, in primitive lands, those who have the least are the most generous. You've no doubt heard stories from missionaries about how poverty-stricken people offer gifts they can ill afford, but to refuse them would be a great insult.

When we come to the Lord, we must come with receiving hands. He has everything we need. We have nothing that He needs. He does, however, want to receive our prayers and praises, our communication with Him. Like a father who needs nothing that his toddler possesses but delights in conversation with him, so our heavenly Father has joy when we come into His presence and bring our requests and needs. He will receive these prayers, and then He will give us grace. Sometimes He grants the requests immediately. Other times He tells us "not now." And sometimes He even says no. But He always hears us and receives us and welcomes us.

Then it is up to us to lean hard on Him and accept His will. Because of His great love, He wants to provide what is best, and that might mean a delay; but He never refuses to hear us when we come in humility and faith.

Yes, we must receive charity from Him. There is no other way to enter the kingdom. It's all of Him and none of us. And that's a wonder we'll ponder for eternity.

LORD GOD, THANK YOU FOR HEARING AND RECEIVING MY PRAYER. I RECEIVE YOUR GRACE AND LOVE, WHICH I DON'T DESERVE BUT WHICH I DEEPLY NEED. IN JESUS' NAME, AMEN.

JOURNAL YOUR WAY TO
a Deeper Faith

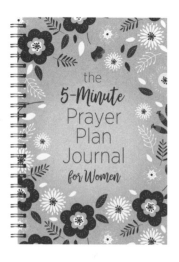

THE 5-MINUTE PRAYER PLAN JOURNAL FOR WOMEN

Many Christians yearn for a dynamic prayer life, but we often get stuck in a repetitive routine of prayer. This practical and inspirational journal will give you new ways to approach prayer with 90 focused 5-minute plans for your daily quiet time. These prayer plans explore a variety of life themes appropriate for women of all ages.

Spiral Bound / 978-1-64352-506-8 / $9.99

WORRY LESS, PRAY MORE DEVOTIONAL JOURNAL

This purposeful devotional journal features 180 readings and prayers designed to help alleviate a woman's worries as she learns to live in the peace of the Almighty God, who offers calm for her anxiety-filled soul.

Flexible Casebound / 978-1-63609-108-2 / $12.99